DON'T SHOOT THE HORSE

('TIL YOU KNOW HOW TO DRIVE THE TRACTOR)

MOVING FROM ANNUAL FUND RAISING TO A LIFE OF GIVING

Herb Mather

DISCIPLESHIP RESOURCES

P.O. BOX 340003 • NASHVILLE, TN 37203-0003
www.discipleshipresources.org

Reprinted 1999, 1996

Cover design by Graphic Matters

ISBN 0-88177-136-8

Library of Congress Catalog Card No. 94-72156

DR136

CONTENTS

PREFACE

Churches need money to operate. This is a fact. A church without money for ministry is like a farmer without capital for seed and equipment: no cash, no crop.

Churches are like farmers in another way too: They need tools, and the tools they use have changed a great deal over the years. At one time, farmers could depend on horses and horse-drawn plows to achieve the results they wanted. Today, most farmers own a tractor.

At age eleven, my brother-in-law hired me to cultivate corn with a two-row cultivator pulled by a team of three horses. The pay was fifty cents a day, plus room and board. My brother-in-law bought a tractor the next year. Both the tractor and the horse-drawn cultivator removed weeds from the corn rows, but the tractor did a better job and it was a lot easier to manage than the horses. I never wanted to go back to cultivating with horse-drawn machinery.

For many years, the tool most churches have used to achieve their financial objectives has been the annual financial campaign—also known as the Every Member Visitation (EMV). Campaigns have helped churches fund their ministries moderately well for about seventy-five years. Even so, the times have been changing. Denominations all across North America are now in a funding crisis. The financial agony is a symptom of deep problems; yet our primary response has been to treat symptoms.

We keep trying to breed better horses. But hanging on to methods that worked a half-century ago will not solve our problems. We have to find new ways to face age-old dilemmas. We need a breakthrough as dramatic as the invention of the "tractor." There is no time to lose!

Let me speak plainly: I am convinced that the day of the annual financial campaign is past. My conviction may come as a surprise to some, since I am employed by my denomination in the area of stewardship. For me to suggest that campaigns belong to the horse-and-buggy era will likely send tremors of disbelief rumbling through temples and offices of my denomination, and will be regarded with deep suspicion by some stewardship colleagues in other denominations. Oh, well. So be it.

What's wrong with the annual financial campaign? In one sense, nothing is inherently wrong with campaigns; they are just becoming obsolete. After all, campaigns (like horse-drawn plows) are only *methods*, tools for bringing in the crop. They serve for a time, but then a different system comes along to do the task more efficiently. (For readers with no farm background, I invite you to mentally substitute a pencil for the horse and a computer for the tractor each time you find this analogy in this book. The effect will be the same.)

The Bible gives no special blessing to old methods. Where in the Holy Writ is the verse, "Every congregation shall have an annual financial campaign"? I can't find it. There is nothing intrinsically sacred about methods. Indeed, methods become demonic when they are worshiped. The past has its limitations.

In another sense, however, campaigns have become part of our problem. Consider: A campaign is a way to fund the budget, but growing a giving church is much more than merely cultivating a budget. The annual "Stewardship Campaign" usually happens in the fall, just before Thanksgiving; but encouragement of giving is a year-round spiritual growth responsibility of the church. In every season, giving is essential both to proclaiming and to demonstrating the ministry of Jesus Christ in the world. A campaign is simply one moment in this larger pattern of personal and communal life. When campaigns are the main focus of stewardship, they become diversionary. They become gimmicks that interrupt the rhythm of the Christian year within the church and distract congregations from their primary task of working within the flow of a giving lifestyle for individuals and families.

The twenty-first century is just around the corner. The time has come to look for fresh ways to encourage giving while providing a financial base for ministry. It is time to build a new system. A variety of methods may be used to nourish giving. Whatever the method, encouragement for a life of generosity needs *to enhance the spiritual development of the people of God*—not detract from it. Our imperative is to weave giving as a joy-filled spiritual discipline into the fabric of the church's life. Just as the farmer plants and cultivates in ways that follow the contour of the land, our encouragement of Christian giving will harmonize with the life experiences of the worshiper.

Imagine that you work for a tractor manufacturing company. You are in the research and planning department. What do you need to know in order to design the tractor? You want the tractor to do everything horses once did—and much more. In other words, you start with the big picture. What are the essentials? What are the desired results? These are the subjects of the first four chapters of this book.

After determining the desired results and the grand purpose of the tractor, your next task is to design specific parts for the tractor that will accomplish the desired results. What are the specific features? How will the parts fit together? Are the parts user-friendly? A discussion of new components and features for the life of giving begins in Chapter 5.

These pages are a compass, not a blueprint. They are a snapshot of brainstorming in the design and development department of a "factory" where the goal is to invent a new system. I invite you, therefore, to join me in looking at giving and church funding through a new lens, and to explore new ways to help people become *giving* Christians and thereby to fund the ministry of the church more adequately.

You may well want to argue with my suggestions. I welcome that. You may even want to challenge my whole premise. Regardless of your agreement or disagreement with the thesis of this book, none of us within the church can duck the issues. The pain is real!

Examine the issues with me. No doubt we will not settle every problem in the course of this book; but we can look for ways to move beyond the limitations of the annual financial campaign in order to encourage giving and fund the mission of the parish for the twenty-first century. Are there better ways to encourage people and to help them grow toward wholeness in their giving? I believe there are! I invite you to join me on this journey to find "a more excellent way."

1

CAMPAIGNS, STEWARDSHIP, AND GIVING

Recent research shows that churches receive a smaller percentage of their members' disposable income with each successive year.[1] As individual income in North America rises, a smaller proportion of those personal funds is channeled into the ministries and mission of the church. If generosity is a sign of spiritual health and wholeness, this decline is disturbing news.

Congregations tend to interpret their shortage of funds as a fiscal problem. It is a much deeper one. At root, the problem is one of spiritual health. Energy is diverted into raising funds instead of into growing giving Christians. We cannot correct the symptoms unless we deal with the root causes.

The funding crisis in the church is not a matter of methods per se. It is a wake-up call to work at the total mission and aim of the church while inviting persons into commitment to the God of the church's ministry. The task before us is to explore procedures for leaders to work creatively and productively on discovering a healthy system for funding the ministry of the church. Let's begin with a bit of history.

HISTORY OF CAMPAIGNS

Traditionally, the annual financial campaign has served a very good purpose in American Christianity. It is uniquely Euro-American and relatively modern. Until frontier religion gathered momentum in the New World, most churches were supported by a governmental tax system. Congregations that received no state support were called "free churches." Expenses were small for these tiny groups. They owned little property and depended almost exclusively upon volunteers to do church work. Whenever funds were collected within the free church fellowships, the monies were for someone else.

A new system of church bureaucracy developed as the American nation grew. The increasing complexity of the culture demanded mechanisms to bring order to the chaos. Church bureaucracies grew to bring order out of this new complexity. Many people will contend that they have grown too much—but that is the subject for another book.

In England and in mainland Europe, most Christians were a part of state churches. Costs related to buildings and clergy were supported through the taxation system. Except for a brief attempt to tax colonists for church support in two colonies, the North American experiment withdrew state support from the church. Giving was primarily a matter of direct aid for the poor, until the fledgling North American churches found that they needed ways to support their buildings, their missions, and their infrastructure.

Furthermore, in the early days of the American colonies, most clergy were single. They received little pay in an economy that practiced hospitality more effectively than it paid salaries. Due to the rigors of their vocation, few circuit riders lived beyond mid-life. There was no need for retirement or health insurance.

As a result of such factors, church finance in America developed incrementally as a pragmatic necessity. Methods developed before theology. Practices went searching for justifications. Connections between Old Testament customs and modern-day practices were awkwardly tied together. Paying the bills took precedence over giving. Laity came to see the financial dimension of church life as a necessary evil. Clergy were embarrassed to ask people to give. We still struggle in North America to relate giving to stewardship, and to integrate both into the journey of living each day as faithful Christians.

An example of this pragmatic approach comes from the annals of American Methodism. Each year the pastor was required to attend a regional clergy meeting called Annual Conference.2 He (all pastors were male in those days) literally carried the final payment of "conference claims" from his congregation to the conference session. During the month before Annual Conference (usually in the summer), the members of the official board of the congregation visited the more well-to-do members of the church. The purpose of these visits was to collect enough money to send the pastor to Conference with sufficient funds to pay the claimants in full. The members of the board who canvassed the members for money were called stewards.

Annual "pledge" campaigns were a practical response to the necessity of purchasing and maintaining buildings, supporting a paid clergy, undergirding missionary outreach, and providing program within a cash economy. In the first decade of the twentieth century, Charles Ward, YMCA secretary in Grand Rapids, Michigan, developed the first Every Member Canvass (EMC). He called it an "intensive campaign." Within a very few years, churches borrowed the plan. By 1910, a fund-raising company was started. In an address delivered in Bossey, Switzerland in 1921, L. K. Thompson reported that "the decade of 1910-1920 saw many communions adopting the 'Every Member Canvass' as the standard formula."[3] For nearly one hundred years the annual campaign worked well. Many other styles besides face-to-face canvassing were introduced, but the EMC has been the backbone of them all.

CONTEMPORARY REALITIES

With this history before us, the question can be reasonably asked, "Why are campaigns now becoming obsolete?" The question challenges us to look at several important realities—both social and theological. We begin with the social.

A few years ago, a respected writer of financial stewardship books advocated a two-and-a-half year (ten quarter) financial campaign.[4] The idea was good. The timing wasn't. The proposal came at the end of an era when bi-annual campaigns might have been generally effective. It assumed a very stable society and a static congregation. It is hard to find either today. We are a highly mobile society. Even when people remain in the same community, they often change jobs several times during their working years.

Congregations once depended on the loyalty of persons to the denomination and to the particular congregation. Neither can be assumed any more. Members of the most dynamic congregations seem to come from a smorgasbord of church backgrounds or none at all. They tend to stay with a congregation as long as that local body of Christ meets their perceived needs. Counting church members is as difficult as counting tropical fish in a large aquarium. Counting on them to *give* is risky.

Loyalty is admirable, but it cannot be the basis for generous giving in North American churches. People still have loyalties, but the loyalties take different forms from the traditional patterns. They are not centered in institutions. Many church leaders believe that those persons born since World War II have little loyalty.[5] The charge is not completely accurate. A large percentage of the generation born after 1946 does not have *institutional* loyalty, but they have strong *relational* loyalties. In fact, they may have more intense, firm, and committed relationships than the loyal "man in the gray flannel suit."

An urban street gang has intense loyalty. Players on a high school athletic team have loyalty. Many clergy have deep denominational loyalty. Some laypersons even have great loyalty to their local church—but it does not come instantaneously. Loyalty sneaks up on the person. It grows slowly. If we were to compare loyalty to a tree, it would be more like an oak than a poplar.

Most traditional annual financial campaigns presuppose a kind of loyalty that is rarely present. They assume a high level of institutional motivation; as a result, they try to bring in the harvest with little or no preparation. They are like a farmer who wants to plant a seed one day and reap the harvest three weeks later. Things simply do not work that way in a field or in the church! Preparation is required in order to bring in a good harvest. The harvest comes from a year-round effort rather than by waving a magic wand in the fall. It comes through day-by-day growth rather than by way of instant maturity.

On the Minnesota farm where I grew up, we went into the fields each spring to till the soil. After the soil was adequately prepared, we planted the seed. When the little plants came up, we cultivated the corn and beans. We considered the soil and climate in deciding what crop to grow, where to grow it, and when it would be planted, cultivated, and harvested. Months after we tilled the soil, we finally harvested the crop.

Likewise, every congregation has an eco-system—an environment that is the context for faith development. The congregation affects and is affected by the larger community of which it is part. In today's social climate, loyalty is a slowly emerging *result* of faith development, not the *reason* for giving. It will grow in a healthy, faithful congregation, but it is never the origin of faith and generosity. A meaningful and effective plan to nurture giving in the lives of people will take these broader social factors into consideration. Let us now examine the theological factors.

THE SCOPE OF BIBLICAL STEWARDSHIP

Along with social factors, there are important theological reasons to question the continuing viability of annual fund-raising campaigns. The basic theological problem with campaigns is that they tend to distort and inhibit the greater purpose of financial giving in relation to biblical stewardship.

The biblical word for "stewardship" (in Greek, *oikonomia*) is not the

most common word in the New Testament, but it is there. It is closely
related to the New Testament word for "world," or "the inhabited earth"
(*oikoumene*). When Jesus used the term, he usually described a vocation.
He told parables about stewards (*oikonomos*).6 They were administrators
or managers of households (*oikos*). They were *not* fund-raisers.

Two thousand years ago in the Middle East, stewards were managers
of the household. They hired and fired. They kept the books, paid the
bills, and made sure that needed foodstuffs, equipment, and supplies were
on hand in the household when they were needed. Apparently, they even
managed the owner's investment assets at times (see Matt. 25:14ff.). They
did whatever was needed for the personal mission of the owner to be fulfilled.

The apostle Paul used the word *steward* as a metaphor. He talked
about being "stewards of the secrets of God" (1 Cor. 4:1, NEB). He com-
mended the treasure of faith to us as an awesome responsibility. All
Christians were urged to grasp that yoke of obligation and privilege. In
the same way, Peter advised us, "Like good stewards of the manifold
grace of God, serve one another with whatever gift each of you has
received" (1 Pet. 4:10).

In this light, biblical stewardship has to do with how we manage
everything in life as a trust from God. To be sure, stewardship includes
the way we earn money and the choices we make about purchasing, saving, and giving—but stewardship is much more than finances. In addition
to finances, stewardship also has to do with ecology, with relationships,
time, gifts, spirit, and leadership.

Our stewardship is manifested not only in how we manage our treasure, but in how we manage our time and talents as well. Some aspects of
the three "Ts" are personal. Some are corporate. Taking care of the earth
is as much a stewardship issue as managing our personal and family
finances or making a will. Talent sharing always affects others. God calls
us to summon the best out of others, while we are invited to use our own
gifts (*charisms*) to the fullest. If the whole doesn't fit together, "steward-
ing" is not happening.

In other words, stewardship is not a strategy for any one of the items
on the list; it is an attitude and a way of life that cares for the whole. In
relation to finances, stewardship has as much to do with how the church
uses funds *after* they are placed in the offering plate as with how the
members earn and give their money.

To provide perspective, consider Diagram A on page 6. The largest and
most comprehensive dimension of stewardship is to accept responsibility

to manage *everything* as a trust from God. Within that all-encompassing understanding, giving money is an important expression. Fund-raising campaigns are simply one method to encourage giving. Neither money nor giving exhausts the meaning of stewardship, and annual campaigns are not the only way to encourage giving.

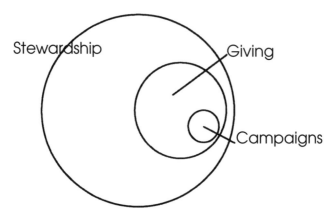

Diagram A: Biblical View of Stewardship

In contrast to this comprehensive biblical model, we often speak of stewardship today as though it were limited to annual fund-raising. In the church, we have sometimes been embarrassed to mention *money* or *giving*, so we have looked for a euphemism. The word *stewardship* has seemed to fill the need.

Many phone calls come into the Stewardship Office of the General Board of Discipleship asking for ways to do a "stewardship campaign." These calls are a sign of trouble. Most congregations conduct annual efforts to underwrite their operating budgets. Technically speaking, however, to identify these campaigns with *stewardship* is not a legitimate biblical use of the term. Indeed, approaching stewardship in this way can even divert attention from the biblical invitation to be God's giving people in every aspect of life.

The distorted notion of stewardship can also be illustrated. Diagram B suggests a perspective within which the concepts of *campaign*, *giving*, and *stewardship* are more or less jumbled together. The method of the campaign actually becomes in some ways the governing reality. In this model, we think of giving primarily in terms of campaigns, and of stewardship primarily in terms of the annual pledge.

Diagram B: Distorted View of Stewardship

In Jesus' time, the rabbi, the seamstress, and the carpenter understood stewardship in its broad biblical sense. This is not so today. Stewardship is an alien word for many persons who occupy the pews in the church. Consider the collectors who pass the offering plates in your Sunday worship service. How many of them will use the word *stewardship* in a conversation the next time they have coffee with friends?

When church leaders announce a "Stewardship Campaign," quite apart from their conscious intentions, they may be adding to the confusion. Most campaigns are designed to encourage those who already contribute to increase the present level of their *financial* giving and to invite new people to begin placing a regular check in the offering plate. If the intent is to raise the amount of money received each week, let's say so.

Ironically, the church may be the only place in modern society where the word *stewardship* is limited to financial campaigns. No doubt the full scope of stewardship is obscure to many persons outside the church as well; yet some people at least use the term in a quasi-biblical sense. In current North American literature, for example, the word is often used in ecological discussions concerning environmental management. As we have seen, care for creation is part of biblical stewardship.

Likewise, the word sometimes appears in a quasi-biblical sense in discussions of business and politics. An excellent book on business management is titled *Stewardship*.7 And when an American president referred to his term in office as the period of his "stewardship," he was using the word in a Pauline sense. Stewardship is always the responsibility to manage a trust.

This is not an appeal to curtail the use of the word *stewardship* within the life of the church—nor is it an appeal to trade one set of partial meanings inside the church for another set outside. What we need is to recover the full biblical scope of the concept of stewardship and, within that, the broader meaning of *giving as a way of life*. Such a recovery will transform not only our understanding of stewardship and giving, but our practices of fund-raising as well.

THE REAL "BOTTOM LINE"

The call to recover a truly biblical vision of stewardship and giving in the church does not necessarily require the immediate dismantling of all annual fund-raising campaigns. It does, however, require a dramatic change of focus and energy. We probably need a transitional period during which the use of annual campaigns is *combined* with the shift toward a year-round biblical process as I have been advocating. During this period, giving campaigns grounded in a biblical vision would attempt to do several things:

◇ Support the mission and ministry of the congregation
◇ Help persons discover the joy of giving
◇ Help persons grow as giving stewards
◇ Support the gospel of Jesus Christ
◇ Bring justice and righteousness into the world in Jesus' name

Sadly, very few campaigns catch this vision. Instead, they are primarily intended to raise funds to meet a budget. The spotlight is aimed at the bottom line. The five items listed above are of year-round significance. What a shame to relegate them to a one-month period each fall.

A college sophomore took a class in German. The professor was a jovial gentleman who had been born and raised in Germany. About halfway though the year, the sophomore figured out the teacher's system. The student could figure out what would be on the next test by listening to clues the professor dropped during the class sessions. Even the final exam was as transparent as window glass. At 4:00 in the morning on the exam day, the sophomore arose and memorized the anticipated test. The student took the two-hour final in forty-five minutes and got an A in the course. Unfortunately, he did not learn German. If he had attempted the test two weeks later, he would have flunked. The primary benefit of the course was a good grade on the college transcript.

We encourage the same kind of behavior in church. The annual financial campaign is a "final test." We prepare brochures, budgets, and letters on how to "ace the test." We train visitors in methods for helping the church get an A or, at least, pass. Too often, we forget to teach giving and faith development in the process. A year-round plan for financial commitment that has faith development at the core can help us grow faithful disciples and build vital congregations.

At the same time, for those of us who are convinced of these issues, there is an important warning. The biblical vision of stewardship is not easy to practice. Those of us in denominational offices often respond to inquiries about "stewardship campaigns" by attempting diversion. We try to detour the caller away from the focus on finances to a dialogue about broad theological issues. We bristle because a perfectly good biblical word is twisted to fit a pragmatic need in the congregation. With a superior tone in our voice, we point out that stewardship is more than money. We are right—but irrelevant. The church is having financial pains. People in leadership positions care about the discomfort. They hurt. Lofty theological talk is not the answer.

We need a new way of describing the "bottom line" in the church. The new description will focus on the giver's need to find joy through participation in the mission of the church to the glory of God: But how do we get there from here?

CONCLUSION

Our focus in this first chapter has been on the need to move beyond the limitations of annual campaign thinking in order to recover a biblical vision for giving as a way of life for the person in the church. The annual campaign is like an old horse. Fifty years ago, the campaign may have been the best way to meet those needs in the church. At that time, the campaign process was filled with vision, but the world is different now. Today, campaigns interrupt healthy processes and fail to produce the results desired. Even when they successfully raise money, they rarely encourage joyful Christian giving.

The lack of generous giving is not cured by harnessing a better horse to the cultivator. The problem is not solved by trying harder but using the same old methods. There is a crying need for fresh ways to look at the matter of giving. Campaigns usually focus on budgetary needs rather than on givers' needs. Marketers offer new campaign models that are really old methods with novel bells and whistles. Too often, packaged annual campaigns help us swap our own creativity in the kitchen of church life for a pre-packaged microwave dinner. All the ingredients may be there, but the meal lacks substance. Fancy candles and a linen table-cloth will not give the meal pizzazz.

In the chapters that follow, we shall be looking in detail at a number of actions, plans, and strategies that facilitate the kind of ministry through giving that I have been describing. Before proceeding, however, let me make an important qualification: Not everything can be changed at once. The transition from horse to tractor did not happen overnight—at least not for everyone. Therefore, even as we move forward to the central thesis of this book, I want to issue two clear warnings. These warnings are not arguments against the thesis; they are simply strategies for leading change in the healthiest way possible.

> **Warning!** We cannot simply stop having campaigns, unless we have effective and comprehensive means to call persons to relate the economic dimensions of their lives to their faith through systematic giving.

> **Warning!** We cannot stop having campaigns until we have a total year-round plan to meet the spiritual needs of the people and the fiscal needs of the congregation.

The remainder of this book is my attempt to describe the pieces of a holistic system described in these warnings. Change is already upon us. The only question is whether we will have a new system in place before the old one collapses.

On the farm where I grew up, we kept horses for several years beyond their functional use. We fed them, but we did not harness them to any machinery. There was no agricultural value added by their presence on our farm. The annual financial campaign is in a similar situation. On the farm, the horses just hung around, consuming food, time, and energy. We didn't shoot them; but they finally died. In the church, if we don't learn to drive the tractor by the time the horses are gone, we will be in trouble. The time to act is now.

2
GIVING AND THE CHURCH'S TASK

Giving has been wrenched away from stewardship in the church. After pulling them apart, we have further confused matters by naming giving "stewardship." To recover the meaning of giving from the narrow focus on fund-raising and to restore it as an integral part (but not the whole) of stewardship, we first need to ask the most basic question, "*Why give?*" For too long, in relation to budgets and giving, we have asked "what" and "how" without asking "why." "What" and "how" questions are not helpful as starting points.

"WHY" BEFORE "HOW"

Dollar sign pragmatism is a poor starting place for the call to give in the church. Financial campaigns have assumed the stance of "meeting the budget." In a financial campaign, however, the invitation for commitment is not likely to be productive unless the total ministry of the church is working effectively. In other words, the congregation's prerequisite to inviting persons to channel their generosity through the church bank account is to be a congregation with a faithful and vital mission.

Business experts tell us that America's competitive situation is at risk because of our demand for quarterly profits. Gurus such as W. Edwards Deming claim that we spend too much time looking at financial goals. If we want to change the results, we need to focus on the processes that embody our vision and mission.[1]

Annual campaigns regularly interrupt or ignore the processes of the church's basic mission. They turn the eyes of church people toward a balance sheet instead of toward a vision. The goal becomes a bottom line rather than a vision of a world where Jesus Christ reigns in the hearts of people and where justice and righteousness are marks of society.

The mission of the church is based on the mission that Jesus affirmed as he read from the scroll of Isaiah in the synagogue of Nazareth: "The Spirit of the Lord is upon me, because he has anointed me to bring good news to the poor. He has sent me to proclaim release to the captives and recovery of sight to the blind, to let the oppressed go free, to proclaim the year of the Lord's favor" (Luke 4:8-9). The mission is similar to his description in the parable of the last judgment (Matt. 25:31ff.). The mission of the church is greater than maintenance of institutions (buildings, clergy, organizational machinery, etc.).

Our understanding of the church's mission has profound consequences. Mission has much to do with how we communicate to those beyond the church's door. The mission either excites people in the pews or lulls them to sleep. A church that is about the business of Christ's mission is in the midst of exciting business.

Idolatry is not only a matter of worshiping evil things; it is often simply turning means into ends. A budget is a means to manage ministry. It is an important tool, but it is not God. Shortsighted appeals for giving focus the spotlight on the budget rather than on the difference those funds are intended to make in the world. National surveys indicate that people in North America find the institutional church more and more irrelevant. These findings sound a death knell for congregations who think their business is simply to continue to exist as an institution.

When we really focus on the "why" question, we begin to remember the purpose of the balance sheet. That purpose is to help us focus on the processes of ministry. The numbers don't give answers; they help us ask better questions. We are called to move our sight from financial figures to people and ministry. The purpose of giving in the church has two dimensions. These are not either/or options. Wholeness requires both, although they teem with tension. They are:

1. Giving is part of an individual's personal journey toward wholeness.
2. Giving is essential to the mission of the ministry of the gospel through the church.

Giving and Spiritual Health

Giving is good for you! This is an aspect of giving that we often overlook. Jesus himself said, "It is more blessed to give than to receive" (Acts 20:35). The New Testament word for "blessed" (in Greek, *makarios*) also means "happy" and "fortunate." In other words, we are made to give, and we are not truly happy until we give as God gives, in whose image we are made.

At the heart of the Christian life is the affirmation that we can have only *one* center. We confess *one* Lord and *one* Savior. Problems develop when we try to divide life into separate compartments. Christianity cannot be limited to faith and prayer, as though it has nothing to do with finances or time commitments. The life of faith is a vigorous, vital, and healthy life. Giving is an essential part of everything we are and everything we do. There is one center for both our prayers and our pocketbook.

When our practice of giving (or our understanding of stewardship) is limited to church fund-raising, we miss out on essential elements of spiritual health and joy. Such narrowly focused giving does little to heal the fragmentation of modern life. Indeed, it may actually contribute to the separation of faith and economic life, and that in itself is part of our problem. God calls us to be good stewards of all that we are and all that we have. An annual pledge of 10 percent does not make us faithful, healthy stewards unless we discover the joy of managing faithfully the other 90 percent of our possessions as well.

As we recover the meaning of giving in relation to biblical stewardship, we shall also rediscover the connections between faith and daily life, including our economic livelihoods. Joyful giving emerges out of gratitude to God. Giving becomes more and more joyful as we experience connections between the money we place in the offering plate and the money we spend for food, clothing, housing, insurance, recreation, medical care, and so forth. Part of the joy of giving in this way is the realization that our lives are moving toward wholeness and integrity.

I am not appealing for perfection. I plead for connection. Life cannot find wholeness as long as we are blind to the relationship between our church life and our work life, our social relationships, and our spiritual commitments. Giving is a tangible act that helps persons make these connections. In a compassionate theology based on the love of God and love of neighbor, the sole motivation for self-giving and financial giving is gratitude for God's love in Jesus Christ. The vertical relationship to God and the horizontal relationship to neighbor come together in the act of giving.

Sadly, just as a center is lacking in the lives of individuals, life isn't fitting together very well in most congregations either. Connections between the faith we proclaim and the systems we use are loose at best. Offerings are too often a boring interlude in a worship service.[2] The annual financial campaign is a "time out" from religion in order to raise money. It doesn't have to be this way. A real focus on the broader meaning of stewardship and giving can be exciting and helpful to the mission of the church and to the life of the Christian giver.

Giving through the church can be a spiritual discipline that assists persons as they work to get their lives in order. Greed and spiritual health in relationships are mutually incompatible. The spiritual discipline of giving can help us focus on the center. Every week, most of us struggle with decisions. The decisions either bring peace to our lives or create stress and injustice.

A discipline is more than an annual emphasis. The need to give and the needs of the church's ministry are year-round. There are many times and places in the natural flow of a church's life when an invitation to give can take place without being an imposition or an appendage. The church's call for giving toward its mission and ministry requires no apology. Financial dimensions cannot be ignored. Our Bible is filled with rules and stories about giving and about the use of possessions. The Hebrew Scriptures describe an annual gathering of the tithes. In fact, there are several descriptions of the way the Hebrew nation did this.[3] There were several locations where offerings could be dedicated. Perhaps that is the origin of variations in giving manuals.

The annual campaign, along with a December urgent appeal, helps a congregation scrape through without getting to the basic issues. The system needs changing for the congregation to work toward a delicate and healthy balance. With an effective system in place, the Christian world does not need to stop for three weeks in October or November for a massive harvest organization in order to put finances in order.

Campaigns focus on the budget; they draw attention to the needs of the church. When a church focuses on *giving*, by contrast, the needs of the giver receive primary attention. Instead of straining to pull funds out of the reluctant giver to support the church, the church becomes the means by which giving persons can fulfill their need to give. In this way, giving becomes incarnational. People discover how the lives of others are affected by their gifts. The meaning of giving is transformed from agony to joy, from reluctance to enthusiasm.

Giving and the Gospel

In a letter to the Corinthian church, Paul developed the case for giving to assist the poor in Jerusalem. He related the offering to the gospel. He said, "You know how generous our Lord Jesus Christ has been: he was rich, yet for your sake he became poor, so that through his poverty you might become rich" (2 Cor. 8:9, NEB). Church leaders often talk about giving in relationship to the needs of the church, but we rarely talk about the relationship of money to the gospel. The connection between our giving (the incarnational act) and the gospel provides a solid foundation.

Jerold Panas affirms, "Donors do not give to critical needs. They give to bold and dramatic opportunities."[4] Think of the practical implications of this fact! Rather than trying to figure out how much money can be raised, start by asking the question, "What is God calling this church to do?" If this doesn't bring about excitement, I doubt that God is in it. Communicate the wonderful answer to that question rather than focusing on the budget figure.

In a study of Lutheran giving, Dr. Edward W. Uthe discovered the same results. He found that "a clear and shared sense of mission and goals among the members . . . [and a] deeply spiritual parish life . . . are much more important than any stewardship programs and activities."[5] When the people within a congregation lack a mission to align their work, they spend their time and energy on internal dynamics. A church without a sense of mission has to be homogeneous if it is to survive as a social institution. By contrast, I am convinced that the only reason Simon the Zealot and Matthew could stay in the same room with one another was their shared commitment to the kingdom (reign) of God.

A common mission provides the possibility for partnerships that appear strange to the outsider. Just because a heterogeneous group is together, however, does not mean that it is a faithful church. The church of Jesus Christ is a mixture of persons with little in common except the common mission found in the good news of the gospel. Diverse people will work together on a common mission. Part of the "working together" in the present economy includes sharing financial resources.

WHAT BUSINESS ARE YOU IN?

Panas interviewed persons who donated gifts of $1 million or more to charitable causes.[6] He wanted to know what motivated them to make those major gifts. In addition, he consulted with religious leaders and directors of development at many kinds of charitable institutions. They told him what potential donors said about why they gave. His research showed that the primary reason for giving was "belief in the mission of the institution" to which they were giving.[7] *Among the million-dollar donors, mission received the rank of 9.6 on a 10 point scale.*[8]

Those of us who invite persons to channel their giving through the institutional church need to examine whether the mission of the organization excites us any more. We are not likely to excite others if we are not excited. Excitement is *caught* more than it is *taught.* It comes through contagion more than argument. If we do not perceive bold and exciting opportunities for supportive community and helpful service, we are not likely to inspire those who hunger for opportunities to give.

Only die-hard loyalists respond to maintenance mission. The biblical call to mission is far more exciting and challenging than a call to pay the heating bill or to support denominational requests. We have a mission similar to that which Jesus read from Isaiah. Jesus excited hearers with words about releasing captives and about the blind receiving sight (Luke 4:8-9). People could visualize the hungry being fed, the thirsty receiving a drink, and the homeless receiving clothing as he told the parable of the last judgment (Matt. 25:31ff.). That is exciting stuff. It is awesome!

What is the business of the church? Some say salvation. Others might say, "To bring the love of Jesus Christ to the world." Frequently denominations and local congregations write statements to define their business. Often the statement sounds like what we think our mission *ought* to be but we may be hard-pressed to match our written declaration with reality. To be sure, it is difficult to make changes until we name both what we believe our mission "ought to be" and what our actions demonstrate it to be in actuality. Only then can we start aligning the reality with the desired mission.

No two congregations are identical. Their size, location, heritage, and assortment of personal gifts are unique. In spite of the differences, each congregation seeks to help people relate to God through Jesus Christ, to nurture them in the faith, and to send them back into the world to live as faithful disciples.9 These movements describe the heart of the congregation's reason for being.

Business management imagery describes a "core process of an organization." The core process is what the organization must do in order to justify its existence. The diagram below shows the four movements in the core process of a congregation. This is what a Christian congregation does in order to be what it is.

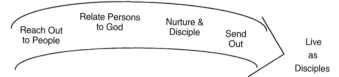

Reach Out to People | Relate Persons to God | Nurture & Disciple | Send Out | Live as Disciples

Most congregations are better at some parts of this core process than others. When one part of the process is not working well, the whole body suffers (see 1 Cor. 12:26). The primary weakness may be called a constraint. It holds back (constrains) the whole mission; it is the weak link in the chain. A severe constraint greatly affects the giving within a congregation.

Constraints are often present even if a church has stated its mission clearly. The statement of the core process helps a congregation identify its constraints. It does not create them. You may want to choose other words to describe the core process in your congregation. You may discover a graphic to illustrate the mission of your church that communicates more clearly. That is fine. My appeal is for each congregation to define its mission. Ground the definition in reality. Honestly name what you do well and where the process is not working well. That is the first step to developing giving among the people.

Finance committees can see their task as support of the core process rather than management of the church finances. Yes, the finances require proper management, but the funds are managed for ministry. The focus is on the ministry rather than on the audit report.

Budgets don't inspire—mission does—but a mission that reaches out to some will turn others off. Our fear of offending anyone can make us so bland that we attract no one. Bill Easum says that "we are more concerned about being nice than with being Christian."10 Every budget is a compromise document (even family budgets). Finance committees have to work at sticking to the essential ministry of the congregation lest they compromise away the core mission. A congregation that has not defined its mission is easily sidetracked. A shared understanding of the core mission can help the finance committee become more than budget supervisors.

CAMPAIGNS AND MISSION

In the stewardship office of the General Board of Discipleship, as mentioned above, we receive many phone calls during the year from local church pastors and from finance committees chairs. The most common question from July through September is, "What kinds of campaign materials seem to work best these days?"

We have learned to refrain from giving a quick answer to this question. It would be nice to sell some of our resources, but there are more important issues. We ask questions. We invite the caller to tell us about his or her church. Finally, we respond like this: "If your church is meet-

ing the spiritual needs of the people, is doing good year-round stewardship education, and is telling the stories of mission and ministry, almost
any kind of financial campaign plan will probably be successful. If your
congregation is not meeting the needs of the people, has neglected stewardship education, and has not been telling the stories of the church's mission and ministry — no campaign is likely to be successful."

If we are doing a good job of ministering to the people and to the
community, a campaign may not even be needed. Without year-round
invitations and encouragement to give, a campaign's effectiveness is seriously crippled. Giving is related to the gospel. The gospel cannot be separated from the mission (or core process) of the congregation. The gospel
is not relegated to three weeks of the year. It is a fifty-two-week message.
Giving is an integral part of the gospel. It is also part of the church's story
year-round.

Campaign methods, manuals, and materials are vastly overrated.
Their effectiveness is especially inflated by people who are trying to sell
them. Let me illustrate with a story from personal experience.

Several years ago, the church I served as pastor decided to use one
of the cut-on-the-dotted-line campaigns (members fill out a pledge and
return it to the church). We used this in a congregation that had never
committed over 40 percent of its budget, although it always paid its bills.
Even denominational requests had always been covered in full. In the
year of the new campaign, the members of the congregation committed
103 percent of the budgeted goal.

I can imagine the author of the campaign materials telling others
how our congregation increased its "estimate of giving" by 63 percent.
Technically, this would have been correct. However, the increase in actual
giving that year was really only slightly over 20 percent. The major statistical increase in commitments came primarily because many people who
had previously refused to sign a commitment card did so that year.

What is more, the statistical change that year was influenced by two
other factors, neither of which had anything to do with the particular campaign materials. First, most of the fifty-two new adult members in that
600-member church made substantial commitments. Second, a multi-
millionaire constituent died during the year. Long-time members figured
they would have to dig deeper to make up for the loss of the wealthy
man's giving.

What was the net result? I am convinced that only about 2-5 percent
of the increase that year *may* have been attributable to the campaign
method.

More significant than the campaign method that year was our decision to ask persons to consider whether their giving was keeping up with where they were trying to grow spiritually. Our spiritual and missional appeal did not even mention the budget. We urged people to feel good about their giving. The church was willing to take money from grouches, but we wanted the people to be cheerful givers. Stories were told of how the funds would be used. People would be helped through the ministry of the church in the community and around the world. Potential givers were asked to make a prayerful decision. Giving was truly related to faith and mission.

CONCLUSION

There is a lot to learn from that congregation's witness and experience. We start with a broad, biblical vision of stewardship and mission. God has entrusted us with a wonderful privilege of management. Giving is invited as a response to this trusting and generous God. The giving is channeled through the life of a congregation that sees its mission as part of the biblical vision.

The annual campaign isn't working very well in most congregations. The financial pinch has awakened us to a problem. The most common response is to try harder. Instead, we need new systems based on more fundamental spiritual and theological foundations. We need to remind our people throughout the year of the connections between their giving and their spiritual development. When people can relate their need to give to the joy of being in mission for others through the church, we will no longer need to worry about the theme for the annual campaign. Mission motivates.

3
LEADERSHIP FOR GIVING

A common workshop exercise from several years ago convinced me that every social group has a leader. The activity began when a workshop "leader" provided several pieces of cardboard, a few yards of string, and four or five sticks to each table group of about six persons. The people within the table groups had not previously known one another. The groups were told that they had fifteen minutes to build a tower using only the materials provided. An observer, watching their interaction, could easily identify one person who emerged as the leader. No outside authority assigned a leader. They did not stop for an election. The leaders emerged.

I made an erroneous assumption about the exercise. I assumed that the person who emerged as "the leader" would be the leader of that group of persons in any and every situation. That is not a correct conclusion. The leader in the tower building exercise might have been the *follower* if the project had been to write a poem or to analyze a system. The leader who emerged had the specific gifts for building a tower. She was able to visualize and had skills to communicate to others in her group. Most likely, she could imagine (visualize) how shapes fit together. If the assignment had called for analytical skills or the ability to write a poem, another person in the group might have emerged as the "natural leader."

Every group in a church has a leader. Some groups elect their leader. Others are assigned a leader. The person elected or assigned is not always the leader in fact. The designated one has the title but the group may choose to follow the lead of someone else.

The laboratory exercise is a simple way to experience something that goes on in every group of human beings — inside and outside the church. The problem is that what actually happens may not seem like the way things "ought" to work. Leadership in the church is called of God and confirmed by the Christian community. It is "supposed" to happen through a process of careful discernment. In real life, committees on nominations are more likely to fill slots than carefully discover and choose leaders. It all happens without anyone—leader(s) or the rest of the group—being conscious of what is taking place.

Leadership is one of many roles within any group. In some groups no one seems to aspire to leadership. In other groups, everyone wants to be the leader. Some individuals prefer to keep control while others are content to move in and out of leadership from time to time. In other words, it is risky to attempt a description of leadership. It is always dynamic, never static.

Persons within any group or organization tend to have a love/hate attitude toward leaders. Leaders are a primary subject of complaint, yet many of the most vocal complainers aspire to be leaders. We don't seem sure of what we want or expect of leaders. When a task is successful, we want the leader to point out that it only happened because of the work of "all the rest of us." When there is a fiasco, it is evident who the leader is. The leader is the person we blame—the scapegoat.

Leadership confusion is a common ailment in the church. The word *leader* sounds so important. It is. The word sounds so exclusive and permanent. It isn't.

Leaders lead. The statement is both true and dangerous. The admonition is a reaction to the movement earlier in this century that advised leaders to always stay in the back of the pack, urging folks from behind but never out in front pulling them along. Leaders were defined as *enablers*. Pastors were not to propose new ideas or suggest plans of action. They were to wait for something to bubble up from the grassroots and then, at most, be a cheerleader. They were to enable persons, but it was usually not clear what they were enabling them to be or to do.

If a dictatorship were the only option to that passive kind of leadership, we might elect to advocate for enabling as the primary method of leadership. But dictatorship is not the only alternative! A whole range of alternatives is more appropriate than either of those polar opposites.

PASTORS AND LAY LEADERS

The Holy Spirit does not work exclusively through ordained clergy, nor are clergy automatically excluded from receiving inspiration from God. Any clergyperson or layperson who believes that God only speaks through him or her is not a leader but a tyrant. On the other hand, any clergyperson or layperson who believes that God only inspires, empowers, and informs *other* people needs to recognize that he or she, too, has ears to hear and eyes to see.

Leadership is not a divine right; it is not an opportunity for boasting. As Paul said, "Not that I have already obtained this or have already reached the goal: but I press on to make it my own, because Christ Jesus has made me his own" (Phil. 3:12).

Church leaders—both clergy and lay—often have a particular fear of leading in areas of giving. The common reason for such fear is that they have never worked through the connection between faith and the economic dimensions of life. Without seeing and feeling this relationship, the only reason for urging giving is that "the church needs some of the filthy money so it can do some good with it." A negative message is communicated.

Don't confuse leading with being "the boss." Not everyone who barks orders is a leader. Issuing a series of orders in a loud voice is not the same as leading—for either a parent or a church leader. Children ignore parents who constantly yell at them. Church members do the same to autocratic leaders.

Both pastors and laity feel confused about leadership roles in the church. We usually assume that the pastor is a leader. However, it is obvious (to most people) that there are other leaders in the local congregation besides the pastor. Each United Methodist congregation has a required office of "Lay Leader." Other denominations have similar offices. There are also leaders of Sunday school classes, committees, the trustees, and prayer groups. With all of these leaders around, in what sense is the pastor a leader?

Some try to define pastoral leadership strictly in religious or "spiritual" terms, but this doesn't solve our problem. Defining the pastor's responsibility as religious or spiritual could imply that the rest of the leadership of the church does not qualify for those adjectives. The lay leader is a religious leader too. The Sunday school is a "religious" activity in the church. Therefore, teachers, Sunday school superintendents, and many other persons with responsibility in the congregation's ministries are spiritual leaders. Indeed, any time anyone leads in an activity, the potential is present for a spiritual dimension.[1] Even the chair of the committee on finance can be a spiritual leader.

LEADERSHIP COMPONENTS

Leadership has four major components: what, who, how, and why. These can be formulated as basic questions: "What does the leader do?" "Who is affected?" "How does the leader do it?" "Why do it?" Unfortunately, the four questions are not linear. In other words, we cannot answer one, put it aside, and go on to the next. They are all mixed up with one another. Each influences the others.

The context of the pastor's leadership is broader than the leadership of the Sunday school superintendent or chair of the women's organization. The pastor is responsible for leading the whole system without micromanaging the parts. Visualize the church's organization as a series of boxes with arrows connecting the boxes to one another, all in support of the congregation's mission. The pastor is not in charge of the boxes but of the arrows that connect the boxes to one another.

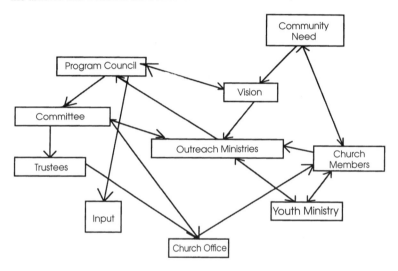

A pastor is one leader among many leaders in a church. Paul's description of the variety of gifts of the Spirit (1 Cor. 12) describes many leadership skills. Some may argue that "administration" (v. 28) is leadership. I disagree with limiting leadership to this one gift. Even if administration and leadership were interchangeable terms, there is no indication that any body of Christ is limited to one person with the gift of administration. In Ephesians 4:11-12, the writer says that the responsibility of persons with several kinds of gifts is to "equip the saints." They are to be equippers rather than doers.

The most common way to describe leadership in an organization is through a hierarchical chart. It is the classic way to describe an organization. The chief leader/officer of the organization is at the top. Under the leader are three to seven persons who report directly to the chief. Each of these persons has from five to fifty persons who report to him or her.

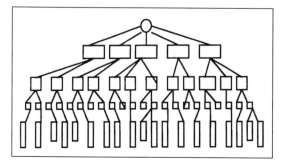

It is not unusual for businesses to have seven to twenty tiers in their organizational chart, although the trend today is toward reducing the numbers of layers in organizations.

Now look at the organized church through a different image. Remember the drawing of an atom in your high school textbook. Each atom has a center (nucleus). Electrons orbit around the nucleus. Each electron has its own orbit, but together the electrons are part of one system.

Identify the "atomic" image with leadership in the church. The pastor is one of the leaders (electrons). The chair of finance is another; the treasurer, another; and the financial secretary, another. Each has his or her own orbit. The electrons orbit around a nucleus. The nucleus is the center. In mystical language, we could say that the nucleus for the church is Jesus Christ. In organizational language, we could call the center the mission, or primary task.

Many tasks are carried out by persons acting alone. However, there are also areas of overlap. All work together to see that the total ministry of the church is enhanced through the ministry of financial stewardship.

This is a radically different "theory of leadership" from the hierarchical model. Most of us have only a vague theory of the way leadership should function. We have a much clearer idea of the ways it should *not* function. The trouble is that we have never thought our theory through to its conclusions. We have not tested it. In fact, we haven't even articulated it. We just keep doing what we have been doing.

A key question is, "What results do our present theory and practice produce?" Try the following exercise. Divide a sheet of paper into two columns. Think of a recent action you and your congregation undertook for purposes of ministry. In the first column write: *This is what we did*. In the second column write: *Here is what happened*. Did the result give evidence that the action was wise? If the paper were presented in a court, would a jury find the theory effective or flawed? We keep doing the same old things because we know how to do them, instead of changing the procedures based upon the evidence.

> MATHER'S LAW: "Congregations tend to keep doing what they have been doing, even if that doesn't produce desired results."

The same image can be transferred to other aspects of the congregation's life and to the church as a whole. The atomic theory of leadership is consistent with Paul's writing on giftedness (charismata) in Romans 12, 1 Corinthians 12, and Ephesians. In certain activities, one person's "orbit" may be primary, while the same person may be supportive when the task calls for different gifts. No one's gift is used in isolation from the community.

THE PASTOR AS GIVING LEADER

How is the pastor's leadership exercised in encouraging and inviting financial giving? What are appropriate styles of leadership? To what end does the pastor invest the skills and energy of leadership? Both pastors and laity involved in the financial ministry of the congregation want to know in what manner pastors are effective leaders in the spiritual discipline of giving. It is a valid question.

When I was ordained, a bishop of the church placed his hand upon my head and intoned, "Take thou authority. . ." I was charged with authority, but that did not automatically make me a leader. Leadership was something I had to earn from the congregation and from my peers. Leadership is conferred by the group rather than assigned by decree. It comes inch by inch instead of by divine or episcopal fiat. To be sure, I had leadership skills in some areas—for instance, preaching—but this did not mean that I was recognized by the laity of the congregation as having any leadership skills or charisma in money matters.

Usually (but not always), laity willingly grant pastors leadership powers and responsibility in matters such as choosing the texts for preaching. Even when the laity disagree with the choices a pastor makes, they usually acknowledge that it is the pastor's prerogative.

The pastor is rarely seen as a leader in the ministry of giving. Most congregations have a committee on finance. The committee has an elected chair. Unfortunately, in many congregations, the committee on finance is designed to hold down expenses rather than to encourage giving. Their focus tends to be on the mechanics of church finance rather than on the spirit of giving.

The treasurer and the financial secretary are important offices. They guide the management of the funds once they come into the life of the church coffers. Few have the time or the gifts for encouraging giving. Some may wield great power to discourage giving. Pastors can affirm the importance of keeping accurate records and sound business practices without trying to take over the details of the tasks.

This does not diminish the pastor's responsibility in the area of financial stewardship. *The pastor is a primary leader in the ministry of giving within the congregation.* A pastor is not the *only* leader for the ministry of giving within the congregation, but pastors have vital leadership responsibilities for giving. The pastor's role is crucial.

More important than specific tasks is the leader's example. Rank-and-file members will not respond to church leaders (lay or clergy) who lack commitment and self-discipline, or who demand that others respond in ways in which they are not willing or able. Perfection is not demanded, but integrity is the bottom line.

Because the tasks and responsibilities of the pastor are so significant, pastors often succumb to the temptation of taking upon themselves responsibilities for too many tasks. Fearing that someone else may "drop the ball," they do things that are more appropriately handled by someone else. Leadership is not taking over or taking away. Pastors need to beware of stealing ministry from laity. Their task is to encourage and, when appropriate, to train or equip laity. Pastors are not ordained to *do* everything in the life of a congregation.

Pastoral leadership does not require knowledge of every detail or expertise about fund-raising. Because few pastors have either, many lay people suggest that "church finance is our business. We will take care of it, pastor. Don't you bother with it at all." Pastors with limited accounting or money management skills are well advised to be learners rather than pseudo-experts in church finance.

Another important caution: While there are some leadership tasks a pastor is called to handle concerning financial stewardship, no one pastor is indispensable to the process. The same can be said for treasurers, financial secretaries, and business managers. Both clergy and laity are

called upon to think of themselves "with sober judgment" (Rom. 12:3).
A class member came to me after a presentation in a class at Garrett-
Evangelical Theological Seminary in Evanston, Illinois. She said, "I
graduate this spring. The thing I dread most about becoming pastor of a
church next year is dealing with stewardship. Today I realized that I don't
have to be an expert on church finance. My job is to help people discover
the joy of giving."

It may not be quite that simple, but she got the idea. The pastor has
leadership responsibility in giving, but that leadership is not primarily in
accounting or fund-raising. Even if that is a pastor's strong suit, the pas-
tor/leader dare not take away from laity the opportunity to use their gifts
in the ministry and work of the congregation.

CHOOSING LEADERS

Financial leadership is important for two basic reasons. Giving is
integral to spiritual wholeness, and money is needed for the ministry of
the church. Leaders do not raise money for the church per se; they raise
money for the legitimate ministries of the church. There is a huge difference between the two perceptions. We are not giving money and raising
funds to perpetuate an organization, but to bring hope, health, and salvation to a world in need. In the present social order that is dominated by
economics, money is a way we connect with others.

One of the ways the pastor exercises leadership in giving is by select-
ing other leaders for this important responsibility. Too many congregations place persons on the Committee on Finance who are capable of
giving generously but who do not give in proportion to their potential.
It is better to have tithers on the committee, regardless of their income,
than persons with great wealth who give sparingly.

Select committed and effective lay leadership. "Job descriptions" for
this committee are rarely thought through. Three factors rise above all
others. First, select persons who are growing in their relationship to Jesus
Christ and working to relate that faith to every part of their daily life.
Second, include persons who are proportionate givers. Third, enlist persons with a commitment to justice in the world.

The first issue is faith. Leaders are not persons who have arrived at
perfection, but they have demonstrated commitment to the faith through
consistent worship attendance and an upright life. Persons of integrity
who are growing in their faithfulness and have the respect of the members
of the congregation are the best prospects for leadership in giving.

The second requirement is that members of the committee be proportionate givers. Do not put persons on a committee on finance simply because they have the *potential* to be generous givers. Placing persons on a committee to manipulate them into a desired action seems unethical, and it rarely works. Reluctant givers in leadership positions have the effect of discouraging giving. The committee on finance is to be a group of giving leaders. They are persons to whom others in the church look for guidance and example. No one can successfully encourage giving without the authenticity of being a giver.

Do not confuse the amount a person gives with generosity. A wealthy person who gives $50 a week may be far less generous than the poor person who gives $5 a week. Since leadership is more a matter of inspiration than numerical manipulation, select fiscal leaders whose actions inspire. Jesus reminded us that a poor person whose monetary gift is small gives more than the rich who put larger amounts in the coffers. (See Luke 21:1-4.)

Justice may seem like a strange issue to add to the list of qualifications for a leadership position in the stewardship of giving. It is important because Jesus related justice to many of his parables about money and possessions. In our modern culture, justice and economic issues are intimately related to one another. A giving leader who lacks concern for those at the bottom of the economic ladder is a dangerous leader.

Justice is not the same as charity. Charity does things *for* people. Justice stands *with* people. The person with a concern for justice will ask hard questions about the relationship of the salaries for the pastors compared to those of the janitorial and secretarial staff. Persons of justice will weigh decisions between expenditures that are nice for the church and those related to serious needs in the community. A person who cares about justice will sometimes make others uncomfortable by asking hard questions. Finance committee members who really care about justice will also work to temper justice with mercy.

NURTURING THE LEADERS

Leaders need nurturing as much as or more than those who are being led. A major responsibility of the pastor is to nurture the lay leaders. Lay leaders can practice the mutuality of ministry by nurturing the pastor in the ministry of giving. They can support one another in prayer.

Pastors are expected to know where to locate resources that will assist lay leaders in carrying out their responsibilities. Most denominations have offices that produce books, manuals, and interpretative materials. Persons with experience and knowledge may be as near as the telephone. They can answer a question or suggest alternatives to a dilemma. Pastors who can make the connections are appreciated by the lay leadership.

A sign of support can be as simple as offering a signature on a letter. The pastor may or may not be the best person to make an announcement. Generally, the lay leaders want the public support of the pastoral leader. In some congregations the laity attempt to get the pastor to be their "gofer." Some pastors offer to be the errand runner without being asked. Pastors and lay leaders are responsible for holding one another accountable for appropriate actions. Give one another encouragement. Thank the leaders (lay or clergy) who take responsibility with faith and joy.

CLERGY GIVING

The most generous occupational group I know are the clergy—not all of them, but most of them. More clergy tithe than any other single vocational group. The strange thing is that many clergy hide that witness under a bushel. They are reluctant to say anything about it. Their silence contributes to the North American taboo about discussing personal finances with anyone.

When members of the clergy work through the meaning of giving in their own lives, they are spiritually equipped to share their insight and witness in appropriate places. It is more important to testify to the meaning of giving in their lives than to recount the number of dollars they give.

Each person has a story. Clergy who are willing to tell their own story of the spiritual discipline of giving provide freedom for laypersons to share their story. Telling the story reinforces the story. It reaches out to others in a nonjudgmental way to invite an exploration of giving.

Giving can be an appropriate topic of conversation in counseling, in committee meetings, and in informal conversations. It does not need to be a part of every conversation, nor is it a taboo subject for conversations. The unhealthy reluctance to mention anything about money and possessions in our relationships with one another is a sign of brokenness. Clergy are not the only ones who have opportunities to help break down the taboo. They do not have the sole responsibility. But they do have the responsibility and the opportunity.

Conclusion

Creative ways to demonstrate leadership for giving are required of both clergy and laity in the church. The invitation to giving is part of the total leadership style, philosophy, and practice for all leaders who care about the wholeness and healthiness of the church and the people.

Because of the variety of gifts and diversity of traditions within congregations, no single pattern can be applied to every situation. Prayerful and courageous testing of leadership approaches and actions will help each congregation discover the joy of giving in its own time and place.

4
BUILDING TRUST

*We must be regarded as Christ's underlings and
as stewards of the secrets of God. Well then,
stewards are expected to show themselves trustworthy.*

1 Corinthians 4:1-2, NEB

The practical results of trust (or its lack) are more evident in financial
stewardship than in any other facet of life in the church. People give to
organizations where they trust the leadership. They will not give to an
organization or an institution if they do not trust the leadership. It is that
simple—and that complicated. You will not buy a tractor unless you trust
the seller and the manufacturer.

In the church, trust is often lost through an act of irresponsibility or
sin. However, it may also disappear through rumor and innuendo. The
results are the same. The loss of trust may be based on fact or on suspicion.
In either case, it hurts. Trust can be shattered in a moment. It takes a
great deal of time to build it back up once it has been damaged.

A major historical shift has taken place in North American perspectives. In the past, trust was assumed. The church and its leadership were
presumed to be trustworthy. There have been scoundrels since the beginning, but they were seen as the exception rather than the rule. That is no
longer the case. Church leaders must now assume that trust has to be
earned. The farther a leader is from the local congregation geographically
and relationally, the more difficult it is to build trust. Many people seem
not to trust anyone they don't know personally. A title or an office is as
likely to be the cause for suspicion as a mark of credibility.

Foundations for trust have always been personal relationships. Paul
wrote to the Corinthians to ask them to contribute to the welfare of the
saints in Jerusalem (2 Cor.8-9). His first step was to let the Corinthians
know that Titus would be handling the money they gave. Apparently, the

churches in Corinth knew Titus and they trusted him. Along with Titus, Paul was sending an unnamed person "whose reputation is high among our congregations everywhere" (v.18, NEB). A long paragraph describes who will be handling the funds and how they will be handled (2 Cor. 8:16-23). Pointedly Paul says, "We want to guard against any criticism of our handling of this generous gift" (v. 20, NEB).

A number of years ago I met with pastor/laity teams from several churches that had been designated as leaders in financial stewardship in their districts. These congregations were chosen by their regional judicatory leader. The pastors and laypersons from each congregation reported on factors that helped their churches become identified as leading churches.

One theme kept emerging in nearly every report—trust. In financially thriving congregations, the people trusted their leadership. They trusted the processes by which the moneys were received, recorded, deposited, and spent. They trusted their judicatory leaders. They trusted the recipients. These congregations were meeting real needs so that people grew in trust toward the whole Christian community.

The most important factor affecting trust in the congregation is whether people are experiencing the inviting, transforming, nurturing, and sending grace of Christ. I recognize that it is impossible to prove this thesis, but I hope I have stated it clearly as well as boldly. Trust comes through the experience of vital ministry. Trust is not so much a matter of facts and figures as it is the sense that the church is ministering to the needs of the people in the pews and in the community. People trust when they personally encounter and observe authentic mission in the life of the congregation.

Budgets are important management tools for the congregation, but they have only limited value in building trust. They certainly do not inspire giving. The information in a budget does little to help build trust, but to withhold the budget from the people will be interpreted as an attempt to hide something. A budget's availability to anyone is a symbol of openness.

PROCESSES

Churches are responsible for being good stewards of the funds given for ministry and mission. Judicatories are responsible for being good stewards of the funds that come to their units. Trustworthy systems are required, so people will be assured that the funds they give will be used for the purposes intended.

Paul told the Corinthians that two persons would be with the money all the way from Corinth to Jerusalem. That practice is recommended for congregations. The presence of two persons whenever money is counted is sound practice and builds trust. It is not an accusation of untrustworthiness, but an assurance that the money is being handled properly. Even the most honest people can make mistakes. Involving two people cuts down the possibility of error and makes it easier to unravel the mystery when a mistake is made. (Involving more than two people can make the process more confusing.)

In our present day, audits are required for most church funds. The audit is a protection for the treasurer and for other money handlers. Trust is a matter of both people and procedures. Auditors are often able to recommend better ways to manage funds. Experts on financial procedures can give helpful guidance on how to improve the system. Improvements in the process help build trust.

COMMUNICATION

Trust is helped or hindered by the processes we use for communication with the congregation. "We are halfway through the year and have received only 46 percent of our budget" is a common cry from Committees on Finance. The message may be statistically accurate, but it is deceptive. Church income rarely comes in at a rate of 8.33 percent per month.

Congregations in resort areas have nontraditional worship attendance patterns. In northern climates, most churches can expect snow or ice to cut down attendance or even to cancel a service some time during the winter months. These interruptions are predictable. In southern retirement areas of the United States, church income is often a reflection of the presence or absence of the "snow birds." Over half of the attendance in some congregations in South Texas and in Florida is comprised of people from northern climates who spend harsh winters in the warm southland. They give when they are present. They don't when they are absent. An African-American congregation with whom I recently consulted always has its greatest income in September. The leaders know this and can plan their expenses around the anticipated cash flow pattern. No congregation receives exactly one-twelfth of its annual income each month. Each has its own pattern.

When a service is missed, the funds rarely come in at the rate they would if there had been an average attendance. This means that the northern church gets behind early in the year and rarely catches up until December.

Monthly Income Three-Year Average	
January	6.7%
February	5.9%
March	9.0%
April	9.3%
May	8.3%
June	7.7%
July	6.5%
August	8.2%
September	9.1%
October	8.6%
November	9.0%
December	11.7%

To build trust, communicate the current financial condition in relationship to the normal pattern of the church rather than in comparison with an arbitrary mathematical standard. Find the average percentage of funds that come in each month by going back three or four years. For instance, in each January for the past four years, what was the percentage of total annual funds that came in during that month? Average those years. Do the same for each succeeding month. Now compare the present year to the average of the past. Report the comparative information.

The "one-twelfth per month" formula may be mathematically correct, but the historical approach gives a clearer picture of reality. In most congregations, repeated desperate appeals based on "running behind" are like the little boy in the fable who repeatedly cried "Wolf!" It feels like manipulation. Alarmism destroys trust in all information. We want to build trust so that persons are free to give. Joy in giving is possible only when the gift is freely given.

DESIGNATED AND UNDESIGNATED FUNDS

Controversy boils within many denominations over "designated giving." Designated giving implies that givers can determine in advance exactly where and how their money will be used. Those who support designated giving are concerned about the abuses of bureaucratic control. Those who oppose designated giving appeal to the need for trust. Both are correct. Givers do not always trust denominational officials to allocate the funds in ways that are consistent with the values of the givers. Those who support designated giving want to control where their money goes rather than put the control into the hands of persons in a far-off board or agency.

People designate giving. The decision to place funds into a church plate is, in itself, a designation. The desire for designation is quite natural. It has many historical precedents. The offering for the saints in Jerusalem (2 Corinthians 8-9) was designated giving. The collection received by John Wesley for paying off the debt on the Foundry (the first official Methodist building) was designated giving. Contributions to capital campaigns are designated giving. Disaster relief is an appeal for designated giving.

In the early days of North American Christianity, most giving was specifically designated. Denominational structures were little more than bare skeletons. Denominational mission agencies and pension funds had not yet been developed. Offerings were usually received for a specific cause or institution.

It was not until the twentieth century that denominations began to work hard at bringing order out of an increasing funding chaos. Standards for funding were to be based on more solid ground that the motivational ability of the person making the appeal. The unified budget was the financial rallying cry in churches between the two World Wars.

Several factors have changed since those "good old days." First, there are many more items on the list of denominational askings today. The past seemed to be less complex. Second, the control of information was less complicated. Fifty years ago, most households had only one radio and no television. The church was a primary source of information. Even though the abilities of some leaders were doubted, their integrity was questioned far less than today.

Also, denominational leaders have taught congregations to understand that mission is not something on the other side of the world but is right on their doorstep. Churches have heard that message and now want to designate more of their funds to mission at home and send less of it to the other side of the world.

Giving relates to ownership and trust. Unless we build relationships and ownership in the ministries of the church, giving will be neglected or diverted.

THE BUREAUCRACY

Local giving is affected by the trust level imputed to those beyond the congregation. Some people in the world make their living by trying to destroy trust levels in denominational and ecumenical ministries. Within the church, our usual way of coping with these attacks is to ignore them or to distribute factual data that tell the "real" story. Neither method works very well.

Church bureaucracy is one of many institutional structures that have developed in North American society. As society has become more complex, bureaucracies have developed in education, in government, and even in business. Most of these bureaucracies are distrusted today. Governments are under attack as "bloated and wasteful." The military bureaucracy seems to be a model of inefficiency and waste. Large corporations have lost their shirt and their stockholders' money through arrogant and detached hierarchies. Church hierarchies are tarred with the same brush. Some of the distrust is deserved. Some isn't.

North Americans seem to hold leaders of charitable organizations (including churches) to a higher standard of ethics and integrity than they would political, business, or higher education leaders. When people place money in a church offering plate, they are not simply contributing to a cause; they are expressing deeply held beliefs. They are responding to a relationship with God.

Church organizations and structures either distort the giver's awareness of God or they strengthen that relationship. The higher standard is to be celebrated instead of dishonored. It is incumbent upon leadership at all levels of the church to clarify and affirm their mission and to reflect that mission as authentically as possible in word and deed.

The appeal of this chapter is to bring everything out of the dark and into the light. The debate may change. The issues wrestled with in a church meeting may be different, but the debate will be about the relationship of the gospel to the world we live in, rather than about privacy and control. Neither denominational nor local church leaders can get away with claiming that they "know best."

Denominational infrastructure is not off-limits for the debate. All denominations are going through a time of assessing what they need and what they want in the way of connectional structures. The number of bureaucratic units is changing. Their size is changing. Most are reducing staff. Expectations are changing. When leaders stubbornly defend the status quo, they are in an awkward position of defending something that may be on its way out. If it isn't going away, at least it is changing!

Few people would claim that the world would be better off with no structure. The debate is about the amount needed and the nature of the required structures. Because most defenders are supported by denominational funds, their defense is perceived as self-serving. The attacks may not be mean personally, but they feel that way to the defender.

LOCAL EXPENSES

If all the money placed in offering plates went to feed the hungry and to house the homeless, our task of communicating would be easy. Most of the funds, however, go to two items: (1) salaries and related benefits for professional staff, and (2) the cost of utilities and upkeep for buildings.

When we use terms and tell stories that imply that the funds are used entirely (or mostly) for traditional mission, we mislead and are quickly found out. Trust is damaged.

In most congregations, about 85 percent of the money that comes into the church's treasury is spent locally. Pensions and insurance are usually sent away, but they are still local expenses. The task before us is to acknowledge the facts and to make a case for the missional use of locally spent funds. If the mission is at our doorstep, locally spent funds may be "benevolent" spending as much as funds sent to a foreign land. If there is need for conversion of the church as well as conversion of the world, there is mission within the congregation.

NEGATIVE FEEDBACK

Negative feedback often comes through stories. Someone says, "I heard that. . . ." The speaker then tells a story he or she heard in a conversation, or read about in a magazine or newspaper, or heard over the radio or television. A common method of dealing with negative stories is to ignore them and hope that the damage will be minimal. In a few cases, that may be the best response.

Sometimes attacks are made that have no basis in truth. They are simply wrong! What are we to do? The answer is not easy. There is no point in dignifying off-the-wall criticisms that have no credibility with 99 percent of the people. On the other hand, we cannot ignore untruths that could damage the trust level of the people. It is a judgment call. In the past, far too many of us have chosen to ignore negative feedback and have paid the price.

When attacked, most of us get defensive. That defensiveness is perceived as an attempt to cover up something. Defensiveness is emotional. Defensive persons usually try to make a rational case. It doesn't work. Feelings come from the center of our being. They do not respond to cool, rational analysis.

In many cases, the most effective way to respond to negative feedback is to assume that people who tell negative stories have a genuine concern. Something is not right. Acknowledging the discomfort can help everyone get to the real issue.

Money is sometimes spent unwisely by the church. This is true of the congregation, the regional judicatory, and the denomination. It is also true of families and individuals. If someone really "blew it," the best thing to do is to confess, ask for forgiveness, and build systems to keep the same thing from happening again. When we try to gloss over something sinister to make it look good, the results are distrust rather than more trust. The question is not whether people in authority have ever done something they should not have done. The question is whether there is a system of accountability so that mistakes, errors, and sins can be appropriately handled. We cannot change the past, but procedures can keep the same mistake from happening again.

In some instances, the negative feedback happens simply because we don't all agree. One person may want to designate funds to fight economic injustice, while another may believe that churches should administer charity but have nothing to do with advocacy. Members will disagree over spending priorities relative to evangelism and Christian education. That is normal. Discussion about substantive issues is healthy.

People do not always agree on the best way to spend funds. Picture a family gathered around a table to discuss the purchase of a new television. One member of the family wants a state-of-the-art 42" projection model. Another argues that a 27" set would make the most sense. A third person believes that a 14" black and white TV is sufficient. Yet another may say, "We have one television in the house and that's enough. I think we should spend the money on something else and I have several ideas."

None of the four people sitting around the table are bad simply because of the differences in opinion about the potential TV purchase. A decision will be made, and all will have to live with that decision as part of the family. The church is a family of believers who do not always agree. We are called upon to voice our concerns and to state them in the clearest way possible, but we stay together as a family.

Arguments often provide an opportunity to examine real issues at the level of the values involved. Most contention takes place at two or three layers out from the core issue. Work to define the core. What are the roots? Invite people to struggle with the core in light of the biblical faith.

CONCLUSION

Trust is never solved "once and for all." We keep working at it, and working at it, and working at it. "Stewards are expected to show themselves trustworthy" (1 Cor. 4:2, NEB). Trust is a lifelong journey and responsibility for the individual and for the institutional church.

Both designated leaders and people who cannot picture themselves as church leaders are often hungry for change. Others may not be convinced that change is needed. The tension between the two attitudes is part of the reality. That tension can be healthy if communication lines are kept open. Trust is built as we join in the struggle to determine what is appropriate for the mission of the gospel in the world today. The old way was simply to pay the askings and to trust that the leaders would use the money properly. A new approach requires much greater participation. However, as with the farmer making the transition from horse to tractor, change is not always easy. Horses come with two ears, two eyes, and four legs. Tractors have many more options. We may not have to shoot the horse. It may die of old age or hardening of the arteries. The problem is, we don't really understand yet the options needed on the tractor. Time may be running out. The time to start building the tractor is now!

Long-time leaders with deep loyalty to the organized church can subtly slide into paternalism. They are sometimes convinced that "we simply must do a better job of explaining our needs to the people. If they just understood that we know best. . . ." For them, working harder on the same old system is preferable to changing it.

They are like the people who wanted to keep the horse after the other farmers learned that the tractor was better equipped for farm tasks. At the root of it all is an attachment to the horse rather than a commitment to growing crops. The means becomes the end—the goal. For too long we have omitted any talk about results. (Jesus described the results in terms such as *the kingdom of God.*) We have talked about the instrument (church) rather than the crop (a transformed world). Let's get to work designing the tractor that will bring the desired results into God's world at this time in history.

5
NEW MEMBER FORMATION

If anyone is in Christ, there is a new creation:
everything old had passed away; see, everything
has become new.

2 Corinthians 5:17

The period of time between a person's first visit to the church and the decision to become an official member of the congregation is a time of crucial formation. If giving is absent from the agenda, both the new member and the mission of the church suffer. The journey into membership is a wonderful opportunity to help persons on their spiritual pilgrimage as giving Christians.

A PLACE TO BEGIN: FORMATION

I struggled with the title for this chapter. Is it *formation* or *training*? Or, perhaps the best word is *orientation*. Each of these words has been used by congregations to describe the process of welcoming new members into full participation. Each of the words includes a dimension that seems missing in the others.

The act of uniting with a particular congregation is an important event. Most leaders want to raise the significance of the experience to the highest level possible. Uniting with a congregation signifies a growing relationship with God and with others. It is a time filled with expectations. The time has come to set aside embarrassment regarding expectations of new members. One of those expectations is giving. How is the new relationship of membership reflected in one's giving? What information about giving do people who unite with a congregation need and want?

The word *training* has limitations. It indicates skill building, obedience, and uniformity. We are trained in how to use a computer or how to drive a car. Church leaders may receive training in public speaking or in the management of volunteers. In one sense, many of us were trained in giving when we were children. Yet I suspect that generosity is inspired by personal example more than it is conveyed through formal training. Many kinds of training are important, but the word doesn't seem to fit what is needed when a person unites with a congregation.

Likewise, *training* sounds a demand for uniformity. Uniformity is desirable in some circumstances. For instance, every time I buy a box of Cheerios in the grocery store, I expect the product to be of uniform quality from one purchase to the next. People who expect the choir to sing on key may be disturbed if the singers can't find a right note through a whole anthem of trying. One man said that he wanted uniformity, but he didn't want uniformly bad singing!

In church, uniformity sounds like an attempt to produce clones. How dull! That is not what we are talking about. We want unity rather than uniformity, and training doesn't seem to get at the issue of Christian community that affirms diversity within unity. Training rarely encourages diversity.

Furthermore, training is often associated with obedience. Dogs are taken to obedience school where they are trained to heel, lie down, fetch, stay, and a host of other commands. Obedience is noble in some instances. It depends on to whom and to what we are being obedient. Blind obedience to a person or to an institution is potentially dangerous. The Jim Jones (Guyana) and David Koresh (Waco, Texas) incidents show the dark side of obedience. Obedience to Jesus Christ is good, but we dare not claim that obedience to the rules of our churches is equivalent to obedience to Christ.

Orientation, on the other hand, sounds like map reading. Some large church buildings almost require a map to get from one place to another. It is usually helpful to take prospective members on a tour of a large facility (e.g., parents of young children want to know how to get from the sanctuary to the nursery).

Leaders escape many difficult encounters if they receive orientation as to where the traditions and other "land mines" are located. Again, orientation is good, but it doesn't sum up what we wish to communicate to new members about giving. At best, orientation is only one dimension of new member formation.

In contrast to these other words, I want to use the word *formation*. Formation is an open-ended word that has as much to do with *being* as with *doing*. Christian formation takes place within the core process of the church. It includes hospitality extended, relationships developed, faith nurtured, and lives empowered. It is multi-dimensional. My appeal is not for giving to be the *only* dimension of faith formation but for it to be an important part of the total picture of faith development. One result of a healthy relationship with God and the church is generous giving.

Formation leads toward deeper and richer commitment of life to God and to the mission of the church. If new member formation were simply dispensing information rather than nurturing and challenging commitment, the new members could draw the conclusion that the requirement and expectation of church membership is to know information. Initiation into the life of a congregation is much more akin to starting on a journey than passing a test. Invite those who unite with the church to respond to the challenge of the gospel through giving. Their giving is supportive of the mission and ministry of the congregation in the name of Jesus Christ.

Actions are always derivative. Doing flows out of being. The connection is important. Unfortunately, a healthy connection is not made automatically. Unless healthy connections are named, the results are rarely desirable. Both good and bad come out of the heart (see Matt. 15:18-19). It is our task to name the healthy outcomes and to invite people to embark upon the journey that leads to health and joy.

Formation also implies relationships more than rules or information. Dr. Edward Uthe summarized his research on Lutheran giving with eight statements, of which statement #7 is, "Knowledge of stewardship concepts (proportionate giving, growth giving) does not make much difference in the amount pledged."[1] Formation has to do with expectations more than with facts.

THE NEW MEMBER

Business leaders know that they have to "know the customer" if they are going to successfully sell their product or service. In the church, Sunday school materials are graded to fit the age of the participants in a class. Communication with small children is different from communication with older adults. The formation responsibility with persons who unite with the church has to be tailored to the uniqueness of the new members.

A variety of persons unite with a congregation. Some are children. Others are youth. Adults make up a major portion of the new members in growing churches. In other congregations, most of the new members are children or spouses of long-time members.

Think of the people who have united with your congregation over the past year. Do they include the entire age spread from children through older adults? What is the significance in the differences in age? Are the new members new to faith, or are they in the midst of a long spiritual journey? Where are they in their spiritual maturity?

Giving is always in the context of larger faith questions. The primary purpose of a focused plan for new member formation is not to pay the bills or to bail out the budget shortfall. New members are being "used" when membership recruitment becomes a plan to pay the bills of the church. In such a case, the church has lost its authentic mission. Giving is an important topic for new member formation because the God of the church is a giving God. We are made in God's image and are created to be givers.

EXPECTATIONS AND GIVING

The biggest reason to discuss giving with new members is because they are receptive. An investment of time and effort in their lives at this juncture is more apt to produce a positive response than an equal amount of time and effort at any other regularly scheduled time within the life of the congregation. The potential return on your investment is maximized.

Most people who unite with a particular congregation enter with a spirit of openness and an air of expectation. Some are openly and genuinely excited. Others are more laid back. The newcomer may be making a first-time commitment to Jesus Christ, or this may be the eleventh transfer of membership from one congregation to another. Regardless of the new member's stage in life or any other variable, there is expectation and anticipation. This moment is an open door. The door may never again be as welcoming to new patterns of action and activity.

Uniting with a specific church is a meaningful time in a person's life. He or she brings certain expectations—which may or may not be articulated. The act of uniting with the congregation has significance both to the congregation and to the new member. It is the responsibility of church leaders to help the new members and the congregation clarify their expectations of each other. What will this new relationship mean? What will each offer to the other? These questions are implicit in the act of formation.

Church leaders have an opportunity to help new members define what it means to be a Christian, to be a member of this denomination, and to belong to this congregation. It is a time to tell the Story and the stories. Clarify the church's understanding of its mission in the community and the world. Define the expectations in practical terms that are within the hopes and possibilities of the new member. As part of the total picture, it is unfair to the new member to omit any word about expectations for giving.

A few congregations name the expectations clearly and without apology. They do so in a straightforward manner and without guilt trips. It is not a "big deal" as much as it is a natural part of who they are. Several years ago, an officer in one such congregation phoned our office. She asked:

"Do you consult with congregations about financial drives?" When I asked what she meant, the caller told the following story of her church.

The congregation was only twelve years old. They had grown from a handful to nearly 1000 members with an average worship attendance of 500. The small rented church building had long been outgrown. Weekly worship was held in space rented from the public school system.

"We purchased thirteen acres of land for a church building. The land is paid for— $350,000. We have another $325,000 in the bank earmarked for the new physical plant. Architects say the building we hope to construct will cost $1,300,000. We went to a local bank to get a loan so we could start construction. The bank officer inquired, 'What are the results of your capital funds campaign?' We asked them what they meant. We have never had a campaign. We just tithe."

Tithing didn't make sense to the bank official. If the congregation was going to get a loan, they had to have a capital funds campaign. The congregation needed the loan but didn't know what to do.

Here was a church getting along quite nicely without a financial campaign (until they tried to do business with the secular world). Is a financial campaign an essential part of good financial stewardship? That congregation didn't seem to think so. The evidence looks pretty convincing.2 Anyone who united with that church knew that tithing was the expectation for giving. It was not a law, but it was an expectation that was communicated in a gentle and loving manner.

The time of uniting with a congregation provides an opportunity to guide new members toward faithful stewardship and giving. A steward discovers his/her own gifts. A steward uses those gifts in the community and through the congregation. A steward uses the resources at his/her disposal in ways that reflect the growing edge of one's faith. The steward reflects his/her understanding of a Christian lifestyle. The steward is a growing, giving Christian. Clearly state the expectations for the giving dimension of total stewardship.

There are many ways to invite new members to become giving persons. If only one or two persons are uniting, the best setting may be a personal interview or conversation. If there is a "critical mass" of people uniting at one time, a more formal series of classes can be held.

TIMING FOR CLASSES ON GIVING

In one sense, any time is a good time to testify to the joy in giving. However, when we look at our church and at our personal schedules, we may feel that there is never a good time to add another responsibility to the calendar. It isn't just that raising expectations about giving is a problem (hang-up) for some people. The problem of finding the time for the session(s) may seem overwhelming. Time will not be scheduled unless leaders consider it important enough to *make the time*.

The most effective timing for intentional faith formation sessions with persons is *prior to formal uniting* with the congregation. Twentieth-century North Americans want to know what they are getting into and they tend to be cautious. When expectations of members are announced *after* new members put their name on the official list, they often feel betrayed. They wonder if the church can be trusted. Straightforward, upfront talk about giving *before* uniting with the congregation is appreciated.

Giving is not the only factor in new member formation. Incorporate a presentation about giving into the *total plan* for new member formation. If your church has four sessions for inquirers, include giving expectations and guidance as half of one of the four sessions. If you have eight sessions, it may be that a whole session can focus on giving.

There are many options for specific times to hold sessions on new member formation. Some congregations schedule the session during the church school hour; some churches may provide a simple lunch at noon on Sunday and have the formation sessions immediately afterward. A weekday evening may work better in some communities and with some people. Explore times that will work best for your leaders and for the inquirers.

WHO WILL LEAD?

The decision about leadership for the formation sessions on giving is a matter of gifts and commitment rather than of titles. The pastor may be the one who is best gifted for the task, although some pastors may lack the particular gifts and graces for this responsibility. Whether it is a pastor or a layperson who leads is not as important as other factors. Choose a presenter who is a giver. Authenticity is more important than erudition.

Select a leader for this session whose giving is a natural expression of his or her faith. Choose someone who finds meaning and joy in giving. Invite a leader who is on a pilgrimage rather than one who has the whole matter of giving "all figured out." Humility communicates a more positive message than arrogance.

Shared leadership by laity and clergy may be the ideal when the gifts and personalities of the two fit together well. Whomever you choose, select persons who are more interested in stories (testimony) than hard figures. It is essential that the presenter be comfortable and unapologetic in talking about giving. The responsibility is to communicate the relationship of giving to faith rather than to persuade persons to support a budget.

Where to Meet?

A sanctuary is generally the least desirable place to hold new member formation sessions. This is especially true if the sanctuary has pews that are fastened to the floor. Informal seating arrangements are much better. Provide comfortable chairs in a circle or a semi-circle, if at all possible. Offer refreshments at the *beginning* of the session. A sense of informality and relaxation sets a tone for openness about giving talk. A rigid seating arrangement hampers openness and interaction.

Holding sessions in a classroom in the church, or in a comfortable room in a parsonage or manse, or sessions that rotate among the homes of participants—all are good options. The aim is to raise the comfort level so that persons are free to raise questions and concerns and to express hopes and feelings.

The Content

The content of the formation session emphasizes witness more than information. Our goal is not to overwhelm persons with data, but to winsomely share expectations. Therefore, the content is shaped by the intersection of the biblical story and the personal stories of the leaders. Both the Story and the stories will be shared in a manner that will intersect with the experience of the inquirers.

New members appreciate straight talk about giving. Heavyhanded, judgmental pronouncements are discounted. Straight talk can be gentle but firm and encouraging. Communicate giving within the context of a person's stewardship of all his/her possessions. Giving is a disciplined reminder of the generosity of God who has given us the gift of Jesus Christ.

Define proportionate giving, and urge people to get on the proportionate giving pathway. Recommend a level of giving that is large enough to provide discipline yet not so large as to cause them to give up. Encourage them to map out a giving plan that will lead them toward a tithe. The most helpful manner of making this presentation is the personal testimony of someone on the journey.

Giving is a spiritual decision. Channeling giving through the church is a decision that has both practical and emotional dimensions. Don't be ashamed to "make your case" in light of the church's mission in the world. Provide solid grounding for every invitation to give in the mission of your church.

There is no one best way to arrange the agenda of a new member for-

mation session on giving. Look at the following outline as one option to
consider as you design the model that will best fit your church and the
people who participate. After each session, evaluate. What do you want
to keep the same? What do you want to do differently?

New Member Formation

SESSION MODEL

1. Open with a welcome statement, a prayer, and a statement of purpose.
2. Have participants remember a time when they gave a gift or received a gift that
   was especially meaningful. Do this in pairs. Ask them to identify . . .
   a. their relationship to the donor or receiver
   b. the feelings involved
   c. the meaning conveyed
3. Ask people to share with the whole group a few of their stories and insights.
   Then remark that our desire is that giving through the church will be meaningful and will provide joy in the sense that their stories communicated.
4. Give a brief history of giving in the Old Testament through tithing, firstfruits
   giving, gleaning, and the jubilee. Then go to the Gospels and note Jesus' parables and statements about money and possessions. You may want the group to
   turn to 2 Corinthians 8-9 to review the message about giving from Paul to the
   churches in Corinth. Accept questions and comments from the group.
5. One of the leaders can share a testimony of his or her giving pilgrimage.
6. Provide practical suggestions for the inquirers to find joy in giving:
   a Give regularly as part of a spiritual discipline.
   b. Give off the top rather than from the leftovers.
   c. Give a percentage rather than a fixed dollar amount.
   d. Set a percentage goal (tithe) to work toward.
   e. When they arrive at their giving goal, they ask God, "What next?"
7. Describe the normal processes within the congregation for pledging, use of
   envelopes, reporting, etc. You may wish to provide pledge cards at this time.
8. Close with another brief testimony of giving and prayer.

When giving is neglected as a part of one's total spiritual growth and
commitment, a distorted image of the faith is communicated. Money is a
powerful symbol of value and commitments in North American culture.
We dare not ignore the use (and abuse) of money in our relationships. It
is a very important indicator of what is important in our individual lives
and in our culture. A relationship with God affects our billfolds, check-
books, credit cards, investments, and estate planning. Faith formation that
excludes economic dimensions is faulty. Formation that includes giving
fosters healthy faith development.

Commitment by the leadership of the church to accept people graciously where they are is not an excuse for leaving people content with their present situation. Point people toward holy and healthy expectations. One of those expectations is proportionate giving. A congregation committed to faith formation does not condemn the person who gives less than half of 1 percent of his or her income. They accept persons where they are and start them on the road toward generosity.

The new associate pastor of a 1700-member church decided to take the new member formation task seriously and to include giving within the process. She developed a series of four sessions with people who were planning to unite with the congregation or were only considering joining. The sessions were designed for people who were coming into the church through either transfer or through profession of faith.

She asked a friend, who was a part of that congregation, to spend a major part of one of the four sessions discussing giving with a group of 12-15 people. The session emphasized total money management as part of Christian commitment and giving through the church as one important part of the stewardship of all resources.

About three years later, four couples from an adult Sunday school class were eating together in a restaurant. The subject of giving came up in a conversation. The man at one end of the table talked about his entrance into this congregation. He remarked, "When we joined this church, Sally (the associate pastor) invited us to a series of classes. She brought in a fellow to talk about giving. I had considered myself pretty generous when I moved here from New England—but I realized in that session that I really wasn't all that generous."

Then he suddenly stopped and looked at the man directly across the table from him. His voice rang with astonishment as he exclaimed, "*You* were the fellow Sally invited in to talk about giving!" Everyone at the table laughed. The new member who told that story had become one of the 20 largest givers in that 1700-member congregation.

Conclusion

New member formation is one of the most significant and most often neglected opportunities to help persons start on the road toward joyful giving—but it is not the only opportune time. In the next chapter we will examine other opportunities to focus on the giving dimension of faith formation.

6

KEY MOMENTS IN THE LIFE OF THE GIVER AND OF THE CHURCH

Financial *campaigns* are one-shot efforts. *Giving* is a year-round concern. In this chapter we look at opportunities throughout the experiences of people and all through the church year when giving education, formation, and invitation are appropriate and helpful. Formation is not limited to a particular season or to the period of time when people unite with a congregation. The Holy Spirit is active in the lives of people throughout the year, year after year. Encouraging giving is a significant part of the church's ministry.

At one time in North America, the church trained people in leadership skills. With those skills, church leaders went on to become leaders in government, commerce, and education. Now the church expects people to move into leadership in the church, having already been trained in the appropriate skills *outside* the church. The same assumptions apply to giving. Giving through the church was a new way for Christians in the New World. The church *trained* people to give. Now we seem to want givers to come with full-blown generosity into the life of the church. It doesn't happen that way. Giving is a year-round task for the church and a life-long growth experience for the individual.

Generosity is a learned trait. There may be a few "giving prodigies" and "generosity savants" in the world, but I doubt it. Most givers develop one step at a time. For many, the journey is two steps forward and one step back. At times it may even seem to be the other way around—one step forward and two back!

Many people find it helpful to write a "giving autobiography." This is a chronology of experiences with money and giving from earliest recollections to the present day. Substantial increases in giving are often associated with times of great joy or great pain—something special happens to cause a change in patterns of giving. A significant event calls for a re-evaluation of values. Rarely do people make significant changes in their giving habits when life is sailing along on an even keel. One reason for hope in increased giving is that few people in our modern world experience life as smooth sailing. Life has many interruptions.

In a research document produced by the Aid Association for Lutherans, the authors state:

> Clearly the unchurched no longer live in a churched society. Churched people say to unchurched people, "Return and be saved." However, unchurched people do not ask, "What must I do to be saved?" Rather, they ask "How can I make my life work?"[1]

People try to "make their lives work" all the time. Sometimes this requires monumental effort. We designate predictable, smooth sailing times as *ordinary times*. During ordinary times, people experience regular, predictable events that are relatively simple to handle. *Extraordinary* times are the major events that disrupt patterns. Ordinary times are birthdays, the seasons of the year, and family traditions in the individual's life. In the church, ordinary times are annual financial campaigns, local church traditions, Easter, and Christmas.

While the ordinary times are not disruptive in the sense experienced by the death of a loved one, they provide wonderful opportunities to "intervene" in the ordinariness of life. Change can take place in ordinary times whenever there is preparation by the leaders and the presence of the Holy Spirit. Easter and Christmas, in particular, provide the church with opportunities to disrupt patterns in creative and helpful ways.

Extraordinary times are comprised of rare and unscheduled events. They include the birth of a child, the death of a loved one, moving to a new part of the country, marriage or divorce, being hired or fired, and serious illness. An extraordinary time in a congregation may be the arrival of a new pastor, a new church building, or a major split in the congregation.

Giving can be developed during both ordinary and extraordinary times. Unfortunately, congregations have fallen into the habit of encouraging giving only one ordinary time per year—during a fall financial campaign. If the campaign is going to be replaced by a better "tractor," we will necessarily discover new possibilities in ordinary and extraordinary times. There are many moments available in the life of the church and of the people for encouraging persons to discover the joy of giving. The list beginning on the following page is intended to be illustrative rather than all-inclusive. Each congregation can make its own list.

BAPTISM OF CHILDREN

The first child born into a household changes everything. Sleep patterns, food preparation, roles, and responsibilities are affected. The checking account ledger looks very different before and after the birth of a new baby. An awesome sense of responsibility flows over the parents of this helpless little child. In denominations that administer infant baptism, a wonderful opportunity presents itself for helpful counsel. New parents review their priorities, lifestyle, and commitments. They may be open to reading a useful book such as *Christians and Money*.2 The birth of a new family member is a time to evaluate financial priorities and to look to the future with hope. It is a time to offer the services and wisdom of the Christian community to the couple. Salespersons will call, urging parents to start saving for college. More life insurance for the parents may be in order. Medical bills intrude upon the spending plan. The parents feel as though they are under siege.

This is a time for encouragement and assistance—not for guilt and high pressure. If there are several families with infants in the congregation, consider inviting the parents to an informal discussion. Let them know that the struggle to meet internal and external expectations may exceed their available income. Provide the opportunity for prayer and emotional support as they sort out answers to questions such as, "How much is enough?" and "What is most important?"

A second or third child provides a receptiveness, but not to the extent of the first child. Parents want to be *giving* people in the broadest sense of that word. Provide encouragement and support as they face the conflicting demands with a mixture of frustration and joy.

CONFIRMATION

Stand at the Wailing Wall in Jerusalem on a spring morning. Watch family units come to celebrate a Bar Mitzvah. The young lad enters the area with his arms wrapped around the Torah and a huge smile on his face. Family and rabbis sing and dance as they accompany the thirteen-year-old to the area of the Wailing Wall where his ceremony will be held.

In our Christian tradition, young men and women about the same age as the Jewish youth celebrating a Bar Mitzvah or Bat Mitzvah often accept the relationship with God as a conscious decision when they are "confirmed" by the church. For some youth, confirmation is a mandatory and boring experience to go through in order to "graduate." For others, it is a time of spiritual growth and maturity in the life of faith. It is an opportunity to review priorities, lifestyle, and commitments. Youth want to deal with real-life issues that matter. Financial commitments are an important part of the picture.

Giving can be seen as an act of joyful response rather than a burden. It can be put in the context of the whole of life. It is a time of defining who they are. Now they consciously choose the designation of "Christian." They make a commitment to follow the God who loved the world so much that he *gave*. Giving is a part of wholeness for those of us who are made in the image of God.[3]

Testimony is a better teacher than abstract facts. Youth will listen to the stories generous givers tell of their personal experiences of giving. Urge the storytellers to witness how giving relates to their life as Christians. A personal testimony is something youth will appreciate and remember.

Few confirmands are going to make large monetary contributions through the church. That isn't the issue. Pre-teens and teenagers are bombarded with hundreds of decisions every day, many of which have economic dimensions. These economic decisions have an impact on every other aspect of life. Help youth recognize the interrelatedness of life. It is impossible to include every decision that may come up. That is OK. The class provides an opportunity for testing and rehearsal. Confirmation is a time for youth to consider whether giving is going to be part of their lives.

Confirmation is an opportunity to interpret to parents the primary issues discussed with the youth. Parents and other close relatives are often as excited about the confirmation as is the confirmand. This provides an opening for the adults to gain new insights and set new priorities and practices. Confirmation is a wonderful opportunity to talk with the parents about what the church attempts to communicate to their children. Ask for their support by word and by example. Their witness and support include giving.

GRADUATION

Youth look forward to graduation. The ceremony itself is not the object of their anticipation but a sign of it. Pomp and Circumstance, mortar boards, diplomas, and the series of parties are symbols of an important passage in the lives of young adults. Regardless of the legal age for adulthood, high school graduates now feel they belong to the adult world.

High school graduation is a memorable event in a time of great change, stress, excitement, decision making, frustration, adventure, community, and loneliness. A large percentage of our church youth go on to college, join the military, or move to another community to pursue a dream. Everything changes.

Graduation is a time of definition that provides youth with another opportunity to name who they are. Identity is related to priorities, lifestyle, and commitments—the very considerations facing people when Jesus said, "Come, follow me."

New choices come so rapidly for the graduate that time is rarely taken to consider the faith resources for the next step in life—unless there is a planned opportunity. Informal sessions (but scheduled and planned) are more likely to be helpful than classes. Invite graduating seniors to someone's living room for a feedback time. Ask them what the church has meant to them in the past. Ask what they want it to mean in the future. If there are several graduating seniors, stay out of the way of their conversation as much as possible.

Ask the young adults about experiences of giving and receiving. Have they ever found great joy in giving? What would it take for the church's ministry to bring joy to their lives about what they give through the church? Raise the kinds of questions that have no pat answers but raise the issues of priorities and values. Pay close attention to the conversation. Do more listening than talking.

THE EMPTY NEST

One Sunday afternoon I stopped in to visit a parishioner. Keith and Edith were the parents of three children. The youngest of the three was a senior in high school. The couple and I sat in their living room. We talked over some church business. Then we just chatted.

Keith described the conversation that had taken place shortly before my arrival that afternoon: "Edith looked over at me awhile ago and said, 'Keith, what are we going to do when Laura goes off to college next fall?'"

Then Keith threw his arms in the air as if signaling for a touchdown and said, "My answer was *rejoice!*" We laughed. Keith was partly right. It is a time of rejoicing, but it is also a time of sadness that requires adjustments.

After an initial modification in lifestyle, the empty nest often allows for a time of great freedom for couples—but not always. And even if it is a time of relaxation and peace, new patterns of life and interaction have to develop.

While traveling on an airplane from Nashville to Pittsburgh, I had a pleasant chat with my seatmate, the chief executive officer for a medium-sized corporation headquartered in Nashville. When he asked about my family, I told him that my wife and I had four children but all were out of the nest. I said we really enjoyed the children but also enjoyed the freedom that comes with the empty nest.

I noticed a strange reaction to my comment. He looked at me with a questioning glance. Later on during the flight I asked him about his family. He told me that his only son had been killed in an auto accident at the age of eighteen. Sadly, I realized that the empty nest is a terrible hell for some people, and I regretted my comment.

Whether the empty nest is a time of joy or sorrow—or a mixture of the two, it is another opportunity to define who we are and what is important to us. It is a time to re-establish priorities, alter lifestyle, and make new commitments. Quite often, the economic dimensions of the empty nest are significant. It is not unusual for auto insurance to go down and dining out expenses to go up. When our last son left home, our grocery bill dropped by half! On the other hand, for some families, the financial strain may skyrocket due to college expenses.

Don't assume that people will be in a position to give more generously now that the children are gone from home. Some will—if they are encouraged to do so. In every case, the church should be supportive of these new occasions, providing new opportunities and unashamedly appealing for giving to be a part of the decision making. Remember—giving benefits the giver as well as the recipient ministries.

Retirement

At retirement, people who found their meaning in life through their work suddenly have a new identity. This new search for meaning and purpose is quite difficult for some people. The stage in life they had looked forward to for years suddenly arrives but feels empty. Everything that seemed important before is called into question.

Retirement almost always requires economic adjustments. Both income and expenses may go down. The specter of inflation hangs overhead like a dark cloud. Retirees wonder if their lives will outlast their retirement money.

At the time of this writing, fixed rate Certificates of Deposit pay very low interest. Retirees are moving their retirement funds out of the very safe (but low return) accounts into equity accounts. Although the return is higher, the risk is greater. They know they could lose it all. What if the stock markets crash? Will they be destitute? The church can ignore those fears only at the risk of ministry failure and financial backlash. The fears are real and must be taken seriously. People who gave generously out of a steady income now see their giving as a risky decision. A pledge is particularly frightening because the "what if" questions loom so large. What if a major illness drains all the assets? What if inflation far outstrips retirement income? What if the stock market takes a major hit?

Every study of charitable giving in America shows that people over 65 years of age give a larger percentage of their income than any other age segment. In 1991, retirees gave 3.6 percent of their income compared to 2.9 percent for those between the ages of 55 and 64 and 2.3 percent for those between the ages of 35 and 44.4 Generous givers of any age need to be affirmed. The balancing act for the church is to recognize the fears without providing excuses for people to miss the joy of giving.

Retirement is an especially important time for the church to help people examine planned giving. Wills and estates can be expressions of faith commitments. Unneeded insurance policies and other tangible assets may become part of one's giving plan. To assume that current giving is the only possibility is to reduce the church's opportunity for money for mission and to deny potential givers the joy of continuing a life-long practice of generosity.5

LIVING ALONE

Many people live alone—and for a variety of reasons. Some do so by choice; for others, it is unavoidable. In a culture such as ours in the U.S., where the job market requires high mobility, one wage earner may even have to move to another part of the country, leaving the spouse waiting for months before joining the marriage partner. Each experience of living alone after a person has been in a multi-person household requires adjustments.

Divorce and death of a spouse are common causes for persons having to live alone. Grief and anger are natural elements of the adjustment to living alone. In addition, new economic responsibilities usually face the one who is left.

Sometimes the death of a heavily insured spouse provides more money to manage than the remaining person ever dreamed possible. At other times, just the opposite problem presents itself—the dependable source of income is suddenly gone. Whether the consequence is poverty or affluence, an adjustment is forced on the one left alone. For some, the adjustment is very difficult. The church can either ignore another opportunity to define who we are—priorities, lifestyle, and commitments—or it can be a helpful partner in the process.

Giving is one way of connecting. People living alone need to feel connected with others. When people are living alone, if not dependent on employment, the giving of time and money can be connected with one another. They connect the person with the ministry of Christ in this world.

Putting It Together in the Congregation

Only the largest congregations can provide specific one-on-one help for every transitional situation in its members' lives. Each local church, regardless of its size, will minister more effectively if it examines the real needs of the people. What are their resources and gifts?

After taking inventory, determine where to invest the time, energy, and fiscal resources to make the greatest difference. What fits who you are as a congregation? The extraordinary and ordinary times relate to the core process of the congregation's mission. The faith community that *truly focuses on the task* is going to help people grow as faithful givers.

Conclusion

The above list is not exhaustive; rather, it is meant as a catalyst for the imagination of church leaders. Look for occasions to help people discover the spiritual discipline of giving. Both ordinary times and extraordinary times are opportunities to help people start a journey along the giving pathway and to nurture those already on the road toward deeper joy in giving.

7

THE OFFERING

The offering time during worship provides the most common opportunity to teach and to invite giving. Pat Jelinek reminds us that "this is not the place to attempt to persuade people to give more."[1] It is a time to help people feel good about their giving.

The offering was a major *festive* occasion in Old Testament times. The writer of Deuteronomy describes the drama as tithes were brought to the temple (14:22-27). They had a celebration—a feast that lasted for several days! Bringing tithes and offerings was an occasion for rejoicing. It was party time in the Temple! The Deuteronomy model is vastly different from the standard experience of the offering in most contemporary churches.

Does your congregation enjoy a party? Or are they "Type A" folks like the older brother in the Parable of the Waiting Father (Luke 15)? The answer is usually obvious during the offering. In many worship services the offering is either like a recess or a funeral, with heavy, plodding music and somber faces. About the only excitement during the time the offerings are collected is when someone drops a plate and coins clatter to the floor!

Friends of mine who have visited in Africa report that the offering in African churches is accompanied by dancing and joyous singing. The people dance their way to the front of the church in order to place their tithes and offerings on the altar. In many African-American congregations the tradition remains for the people to individually bring their tithes and offerings to the altar. Unfortunately, the dancing has disappeared. People march to the altar with the air of someone going to view a casket at a wake. The form is still there, but the power and joy have disappeared.

Giving is an important spiritual discipline. Ways can be found to make the offering much more inspiring and exciting. Almost any form can become routine and drab, but the challenge before the contemporary church is to discover symbols and actions that will communicate gratitude and joy.

Worship traditions are so ingrown in most congregations that any changes in the way we give and receive offerings are most likely to come from the youth. Turn their imaginations loose! Ask them what would make the offering meaningful as an act of joyful response to a generous God. Following is an example of a creative way to dedicate offerings:

When the offerings of the people are brought to the altar for dedication, a family unit comes from the pews to offer the dedicatory prayer. The family symbolizes the dedication of the offerings on behalf of the whole church.

Sometimes the family unit is one person. Other times it may be a couple with children, or a single parent, or a blended family. The selection of families symbolizes the inclusiveness of the congregation.

In order to counteract the deadliness of the offering in a worship service, a radical option is to *stop passing the plates*. A regional staffperson told me about a congregation in Maryland where "they never take an offering." That so aroused my curiosity that I called the pastor.[2] He said, "Yes. We stopped passing the plates three years ago." I asked what led to the decision and what the results were.

Several factors led to the decision. Boredom was one element, but not the most important one. The primary concern of the leaders was *the witness made to newcomers*. The church is growing, with new people visiting almost every Sunday. Many of them have not been in church for ten to fifteen years. If they ever received training in living and giving, it is long forgotten.

The pastor describes the typical scenario *before* changing their way of handling the offering:

The plate was passed by those in the pew in front of where visitors were seated. The visitors wondered what to put in the plate. They looked at what others were doing as a cue for what was expected from them.

The family in the pew in front of them put a $1 bill in the plate. (A typical regular attender is paid once a month, so he writes a check to the church after his

---

employer deposits funds into his personal bank account by electronic mail. Still, something inside him makes him feel as if he should put an additional amount in the plate when it goes by. This is not the Sunday for the check, so a $1 bill goes in.)

Our newcomer saw the $1 bill go into the plate and assumed that a $1 contribution was the standard amount— at least for those who didn't have envelopes.

Members of the church said, "We are giving a terrible witness when we put a $1 bill in the plate. $1 isn't worth anything. We know it. The newcomer knows it. We don't want to trivialize the faith that way."

The church now mails envelopes to members each month. Offering plates are kept at each entrance and exit. The first year the congregation stopped passing the plates in the service, the loose plate collection went up 300 percent. Apparently, those who put money in the plate now put in $5 and $10 bills rather than singles.

A congregation in New York State that heard about the Maryland church decided they would stop passing the plates too. Giving dropped precipitously because they did not have systems in place to encourage giving. *They shot the horse before they knew how to the drive the tractor.* The decision to stop passing the plates was a gimmick for them, and like most gimmicks, it didn't work.

HISTORY

A manuscript came to my desk from a pastor in Georgia.[3] In it he described the entrepreneurial evangelists who rode up and down the Eastern seaboard during the colonial days in America, proclaiming the gospel with passion. In addition to proclaiming the gospel, they started schools, orphanages, and hospitals. This required substantial financial resources, so they took up offerings at every preaching opportunity. That is the way the tradition began of receiving a monetary offering at every worship service.

Early congregations in the New World got their funds primarily through pew rents. Although widely used, the practice had detractors from the beginning. One denomination took its name from its opposition to the practice—the Free Methodists. They did not think people should have to pay for a place to sit in the sanctuary. Pew rents discriminated against the poor.

Wishing to know more of the origins of the practice of passing the plate, I went to the best authority I know on worship. Hoyt L. Hickman proved to be a walking encyclopedia of knowledge.[4] When I asked him when passing the plates began, he said, "Offerings are a 200-year-old American phenomenon."

I asked, "What about the offertory in a worship service? Hasn't it been around since the early days of Christianity?"

"Yes," said Hoyt, "but it had nothing to do with money. The offertory was the time in the Mass when the bread and wine were 'offered' to God for sanctification."

Cyril Richardson describes this sacramental offering as follows:

> Each Christian brought some bread and wine and this was collected by the deacons and consecrated by the bishop or elders, so that the united offerings of the people became one sacrament. At the Eucharist they also gave freely of their substance (in kind as well as in money) for the aid of the shipwrecked sailors, orphans, widows, captives, and unemployed. All Christians in need were cared for and nourished from this liberal treasury. Their corporate devotion and their practical life of love were knit together in real unity.[5]

The offering was a symbol of their faith, their compassion, and their unity. We have turned the offering into a practical means of collecting money to pay the bills. Until the symbolic power of the offering is returned, it is unlikely that joy will be evident in the action. The offering is an opportunity to help people make the connection between faith and living. Giving has the potential for being a response to God who gave and who continues to give.

VARIETIES OF OFFERINGS

In the Old Testament there were many different kinds of offerings. Some were to take away sin. Others were to consecrate a person such as Aaron (Exod. 29) or to consecrate a place such as Shechem (Gen. 12:4-9). Some offerings were to thank God for a victory or for a promise fulfilled. People made offerings to ask God's favor or to remember a meaningful event.

One kind of offering is called the *votive offering*. This is a one-time gift expressing gratitude. Contemporary Korean brothers and sisters have emphasized this gratitude giving in an enthusiastic manner. In most Korean congregations, the people look for ways to make a gratitude (votive) offering.

Many years ago in a large church in Colorado Springs, Colorado, I found a card in the pew rack that invited people to make gratitude offerings. It looked something like this:

☐ We/I wish to make a special gratitude offering in the
   amount of $_____

This signifies: _____ a birthday
                  _____ an anniversary
                  _____ an inheritance
                  _____ a tax refund
                  _____ other

or in honor of (*please name*)
                  _____ family member
                  _____ friend
                  _____ other

☐ We/I wish to increase the amount we regularly give to the
   ministries of this congregation.
☐ Our new level of giving will be $_____ per week/month/year.

Name _____

Address _____

Phone _____

Another frequent kind of offering noted in the Old Testament was a free-will offering, a spontaneous gift that usually comes out of compassion and caring. When we hear of devastation caused by a natural disaster, such as a flood or earthquake, and see the images on our television screens, we want to help. An opportunity for an offering on the following Sunday is an example of a free-will offering.

A few church leaders (both pastors and lay financial leaders) try to protect people from free-will offerings. There is a myth that money given in a free-will offering will be taken away from the funds needed to "pay the bills." In almost every case the opposite is true: Giving begets giving. Free-will offerings are special opportunities to teach the joy of giving. They are an open invitation to test the waters of glad giving.

Giving Patterns

Just as there are predictable variations from month to month, giving tends to follow a consistent pattern for each week of the month.[6] Most congregations receive more funds the first Sunday of the month than on successive Sundays. Fifth Sundays usually bring in the smallest offerings. There are at least two explanations for the larger offerings on the first Sundays. The first reason is the large number of retirees in many congregations. They receive their Social Security payments on the 3rd of each month. Many of these people tithe their income and follow the tradition of "paying off the top." The first check they write is their tithe. The result is a larger offering at the beginning of the month.

Many people are paid once or twice a month. In either arrangement, the first Sunday of the month is immediately after a payday. The pattern of giving is largely determined by when the money is deposited into the members' personal accounts. Income patterns strongly affect giving.

People who give their offering the next Sunday after receiving the income are following the concept of "firstfruits giving" in the Old Testament.[7] The practice of giving the first lamb, the first bushel of grapes, or the first sheaves of wheat meant that people gave in faith rather than giving from leftovers. The pattern of giving immediately after funds are received is a sign of giving health rather than a matter for concern. Explore creative ways for people to participate in the offering, even when it is not "their Sunday" to put their check in the plate. No one should feel excluded.

Another kind of giver may feel left out when the plate is passed. This is the person who is self-employed and receives a delayed, irregular income. Farmers, manufacturer's representatives (salespersons), stock brokers, real estate agents, freelance artists, and a host of others are never sure what their net income will be at the beginning of the year. If they make a "pledge," they probably estimate on the low side—to "hedge their bets," so to speak. Their income may come primarily at one time during the year, rather than being evenly spaced throughout.

In most congregations, the way the offering is introduced neglects to provide an opportunity for generosity by persons who just had a strong economic week. It makes the same people feel guilty if the week produced little or no income. Variation in giving makes budget watchers anxious, but the fluctuation is not necessarily a sign of a lack of commitment or of sin.

Since patterns are fairly predictable within any particular congregation, the finance committee can plan expenditures in a way that allows for normal cash flow variations. This will help reduce guilt-inducing articles in the church newsletter and panic appeals when they are not necessary. Recognition of patterns will affect the way financial officials report to official meetings of the church. A report on the basis of normal patterns of income flow will give a more accurate picture than the usual one-twelfth-per-month reports that convey a negative message. If the news really is bad, it needs to be reported. If there is improvement on a comparative basis from previous years, celebrate the growth.

DIRECT BANK DEBIT

An increasing number of churches provide people with the option of giving to support the ministry and mission of the church through electronic fund transfer directly from their personal account to the church's bank account. There is usually a small charge for this transaction. A finance committee can talk to local bank officials about arrangements required to offer this option.

Recently I had a conversation with a peer about direct bank debit. Her instant response was, "Wow! That's real commitment." The practice never struck me that way. However, when we consider how many people live to the limit of their bank account each month, many of whom do not keep very good track of their checks, it may be a significant act of commitment. The practice of giving through electronic fund transfer may help people bring discipline to all of their income and expenses.

Churches that offer this option and continue to pass the plates during a worship service need to provide a way for the electronic givers to participate in the offering segment of the worship service. The simplest way to do this is to provide an offering "card."

This represents our contribution to the ministry of

CHRIST CHURCH

through the electronic transfer of funds from our bank

Givers may place such a card in the offering plate each time the plate is passed, symbolically participating in the act of worship as fully as the person who places a check in the plate.

Sacramental Giving

The offering is not primarily a mechanical convenience to gather funds to support the budget of the church. It is intended as *an act of worship*. The story of the first Passover in Exodus 12 is an instructive model for the offering. Each family provided a lamb for sacrifice. The lamb was material . . . real . . . of value. It was to be treated in a special way—to be "set aside." It is obvious that the lamb was significant beyond simply being a lamb. The givers were asked to remember a particular historical act that gave them identity and life. The remembering produced gratitude.

The lamb was eaten. The meal prefigures the Eucharist for Christians. The act was therefore communal. The act was for the whole nation rather than an individual attempt to get right with God.

The offerings we make are real. A portion of a person's total resources is set aside for this holy act. It is a symbol of remembrance that *all we have and all we are* ultimately comes from God. We usually "gift wrap" them in envelopes. The offering is handled in a special way. The ritual of passing the plates, bringing the plates forward for consecration, and the prayer of dedication "set aside" this money.

The offering is communal in that it is an action of the people of God when they come together in worship. Finally, it is an act of gratitude. God has acted in Jesus Christ. "God so loved the world that (God) gave . . ." (John 3:16). That supreme act and all other acts of God's giving love are remembered when we participate in the offering in our churches.

Participation in this communal act does not end with the passing of the plates in the pews. The act is consummated at the altar table with a gesture of praise and of gratitude. In several traditions, the pastor receives the plates, goes to the altar table, and raises the plates high as the congregation sings a doxology. That drama is a way to bring the action to an appropriate climax.

Conclusion

The offering is invitation, celebration, and convenience. It provides an opportunity for people to physically act out a spiritual discipline and, at the same time, participate in the mission and ministry of the church. The relatively modern act is rooted in tradition. Changing from a "horse" to a "tractor" in this case may actually put us in touch with older and deeper traditions. New ways to receive offerings can be both spiritually fulfilling and easy to use.

8
TELLING STORIES

Jesus told stories we call *parables*. These stories are easily remembered and communicate far more effectively than statistical data can ever approximate. Good stories can be told and retold without putting people asleep. Each retelling has the potential for conveying new insight.

Stories continue to be an important way to communicate. Many good preachers are excellent storytellers. Excellent stories have the power to both inspire and trouble. Elementary-age children are as likely as the Ph.D. to understand a good story. A well-told story is a picture that tells much more than a million bits of hard data.

Stories can build up or they can tear down. They must be used wisely, tenderly, and lovingly. The tone of voice of the storyteller is as important as the information in the story itself. Read aloud the opening verses of 2 Corinthians 8—once with a voice filled with anger and threat, then as an inspiring tale of encouragement. The tone of voice conveys a dramatically different message and stirs up a very different response.

Facts are not evils. They are simply uninspiring (non-*spirit*-ing). There is no life in them; they are dry bones. To live in the hearts and minds of the people, the dry bones of facts have to be clothed with flesh and blood. The breath of life vibrates within them.

Money is important to the people of the church (and to others). Givers want to know that money placed in the offering plate is going to be used for good. They want their giving to have a positive effect on the lives of people in their own community and around the world. How can they know unless someone tells them? The most effective way to describe the impact of money upon people is through stories. Tim Bagwell reminds us that Jesus "helped people picture the kingdom of God, and he invited them to see themselves in the picture. He relied on stories to make his point."[1]

The more human and personal the stories are, the better they will communicate. Give the stories life. Help them breathe with passion and excitement. That doesn't mean that you make up fictitious stories. However, the need for authenticity doesn't require that all imagination be removed. Truth is not contrary to facts. Through stories, truth is connected to people's lives.

DEALING WITH NEGATIVE FEEDBACK

The church does not control all stories heard by rank-and-file members or by leaders. Many of the stories come from secular sources outside the congregation. Some can be very helpful. When the evening television news graphically shows the destruction from a flood, hurricane, or earthquake during the week before the church receives a special offering to aid victims, generous giving is supported by the portrayal.

Some stories are *not* helpful. They create doubt and suspicion. They question the judgment of leadership and the use of funds. It is not easy to know how to respond to negative stories.

For starters, we can acknowledge that sometimes the church does inappropriate things. Sometimes it does wrong things. If funds have been used in an improper manner, confess the sin rather than trying to rationalize it. Excuses dig the hole deeper and deeper. Ask for forgiveness and leave it there.

Urge people to make a case for their values in their local congregation as well as with the financial leaders of the judiciary. Provide information so that concerned people can study the issue and present an informed argument. The process has the opportunity to provide learning and growth. The process may turn out to be a story in itself.

After a recent attack on old-line churches by *Reader's Digest*, a pastor came down from the pulpit and spoke directly to the people. The gist of what he said follows:

> When our enemies are attacked, we usually ignore it—or we might even smile. When *our* ox is gored, it hurts. I have seen the article in the *Reader's Digest* that attacks our denomination and some of the ecumenical organizations with whom we relate. It doesn't feel good. I am not going to try to straighten the record this morning. I don't have the facts. I know that we are not above criticism. I also believe that much of what is in the article is unfair or just plain wrong. They have raised some questions that we need to face. If any of you are interested in trying to find out more, I invite you to join me in getting more informa-

tion about the charges. At this point, I urge all of you to
withhold judgment until we have an opportunity to look at
the attack from all sides. For today, let us all admit that it
hurts.

The pastor did an effective job of addressing the feelings rather than
becoming defensive about unfair attacks. He built trust that day. Without
ignoring the facts, the pastor responded primarily to the feelings. Feelings
relate to values. An avalanche of facts would have felt like a discounting
of the values of some of the people.

Many years ago, some members of a church where I was pastor felt
very strongly about the World Council of Churches. (They were against
it.) I responded to their suspicion and doubt with this story.

> While a seminary student, I worked part-time with the
> youth program in a church in Bloomfield, New Jersey. In
> February of my final academic year, the 41-year-old-senior
> pastor, Bob Ramm, developed a brain tumor and died less
> than a week after the diagnosis. I spent several days at
> the hospital beside his bed. Every day, a friend of Bob's
> came to visit. The visitor was a tower of spiritual strength in
> the midst of hovering death. His prayers brought peace to
> my heart. His counsel to Bob's wife and to me was faith-
> filled and communicated confidence in God's grace.
> The man was Eugene Smith, a top executive of the World
> Council of Churches. Whenever I think of that organiza-
> tion, I think of Dr. Smith. I don't know about the specific
> charges you have heard but I experienced one of their
> top leaders to be one of the most faith-filled persons I
> have ever met.

I shared my feelings rather than defending an organization. I was
fortunate to have a personal testimony with which to respond to negative
accusations about the way the donations of the people were being used.
Facts would not have addressed the feelings expressed by those who
opposed the organization. Facts can be doubted.

A personal testimony is the most effective story. It makes no charges.
It does not argue. It describes feelings and bases them in personal experience. Even if you do not have a testimony to share that is relevant to a
particular concern, search for a story that communicates feelings rather
than facts.

Giving and Stories

About forty pastors gathered for a seminar. The subject was "How to increase missional giving in the church." The leader gathered the group into groups of four and gave them this assignment: "Review the list of denominationally apportioned funds. Choose two items on that list that you feel good about. The only rule is that you may not name pensions or insurance."

The groups huddled for about five minutes, then were asked to report their lists. Only two of the ten groups named items they affirmed among the denominational list. The rest could not name any denominational fund that they felt good about. It is no wonder that giving was a problem in that area. When leaders have no enthusiasm and no stories, giving is rarely joyful or generous.

Stories inspire giving. When the people charged with sharing stories don't know any—or believe that there are none—inspired giving is not very likely.

Let's not confuse stories with facts. Denominations do a good job of producing fact sheets. Pie charts and line item budgets are relatively easy to get from most church organizations. The problem is that they are boring. They do not inspire. They create a ho-hum response.

Stories, on the other hand, grab attention, stir the imagination, and paint pictures. They build relationships that create a desire to become involved. One of the doorways to involvement in a capitalistic society is through financial participation and giving.

Jesus said, "Go out into the roads and lanes, and compel people to come in, so that my house may be filled" (Luke 14:23). It is not likely that he meant that we should use strong-arm tactics, but that the combination of our excitement and the story would be such that people would feel they had to be at the banquet. That is the idea behind the stories. Combine excitement with the stories in such a way that there is a "compelling reason" to give.

Stories That Say "Thank You"

Stories are also part of the feedback loop. Geoff and Helene give very generously through their church. Their tithe amounts to over $5,000 a year. Ninety percent of that amount is given directly into the budget of their local congregation.

The generous giving of Geoff and Helene does not, however, give them the right to dictate the ministry and mission of the church. It does not even give them the right to choose the paint color for the sanctuary. But they do deserve to hear stories of the difference their giving is making in the community and in the world. What, in Christ's name, is done with the money that is put in the plate? Tell the story in human terms.

Sometimes feedback comes prior to the giving. We can thank in advance. That is what Paul did in his fund-raising letter to the Corinthian church (2 Cor. 8, NEB), "Let me tell you . . . about the grace of generosity . . . in Macedonia." He bragged on the Macedonians. He praised the Corinthians for their commendable qualities and indicated that he wanted to add generosity to the list (v. 7).

Giving is not a means for getting appreciation. Appreciation is a gift given to the giver. It is not the giver's responsibility to ask for a thank you. It is the church's responsibility to say thank you to all who give. Stories lead people to the door and subtly raise the joy level for those who have already entered the household of givers. A thank you is more than a common courtesy; it is a rightful reward.

DIFFERENT STORIES FOR DIFFERENT FOLKS

Even when people agree on a subject, not all may be impressed with the same message. Stories are closer to being universal than hard data, but even excellent stories have their limitations. No one story will reach everyone. A little experiment will illustrate.

Select four quarter-page to half-page stories of ministries of your congregation and/or of the denomination. For instance, you could choose:

◇ A story about an inner-city ministry
◇ A story about an agricultural mission in Africa
◇ A story of disaster relief
◇ A story of evangelical outreach in India

Make copies of the stories and give them to separate groups of youth, young adults, middle adults, and older adults. Ask each person to tell which story is most inspiring. "Which story would make you want to open your checkbook or wallet?"

> Listen to the people within the groups talk about why they selected their particular stories. You will learn a great deal about what communicates.
> Note any differences in the response by age. Are differences related to theological stance? To the respondent's economic situation? To the family relationship? To length of time the person has been a part of the congregation? Is there a difference in what appeals to men and to women? There may be other differentiations.

The information you receive from your experiment provides important data on effective communication with your congregation. Have a group of persons interpret the data and recommend actions to respond to the insights.

Different people are inspired by different stories. In a helpful book by Warren Hartman (*Five Audiences*), the author shows how different segments of the congregation react to everything from the teaching subject and style in a Sunday school class to the nature of the worship service.[2]

Leaders tend to choose the stories that are most meaningful to them personally. That is all right as long as a substantial portion of the congregation is inspired by the same things. Even so, in any group there are a few people who are different from the leader (gender, age, race, economic class). Include them too. Provide a variety of stories.

The same stories are not likely to be meaningful for the non-giver as for the generous giver. When a non-giver hears a testimony by a long-standing tither, the context may not connect. It sounds nice, but the story is from a different world. Help the non-givers get into the giving world before trying to inspire them to be generous givers.

Action Suggestions

The first rule of "doing it" is to do it regularly. Keep the stories flowing year-round, and use every means available. An intensive barrage of stories during a fall financial campaign will not make up for the neglect of the previous eleven months.

Most stories communicate better orally than in print. Nevertheless, include stories of the mission and ministry of your congregation and denomination in newsletters and other print communication mediums. Homebound people tend to read every word that comes from their church.

Inactives rarely read the stories they receive through the mail. Even though the story arrives in their mailbox, it is not likely to be received in their hearts. Monthly letters written by a variety of persons within the congregation are an effective way of telling stories. Select twelve members of the congregation, and invite each one to write a letter during the year to communicate a witness about giving or an insight into the ministry of the congregation. People love to read letters written by people they know. A full description of this method of communication is found in the book, *Letters for All Seasons*.3

The sermon is a wonderful time to tell stories that inspire giving. Don't limit this emphasis to the time of annual financial giving. Advent is a natural season of the year to tell stories of giving. Connect the texts to real life through stories. When the story has a direct link to your congregation, name the connection for the people.

Timothy Bagwell describes the "right-brained" way of preaching in his excellent book, *Preaching for Giving*.4 Through word pictures and examples, he helps the preacher see the way to the imagination of the hearer in the pew. In Charlie Shedd's book titled, *The Exciting Church: Where They Give Their Money Away*,5 the author describes ways to communicate the stories of the church's outreach visually as well as orally. Give dramatic descriptions that affirm ways your congregation lives the message of Luke 4:18-19, where Jesus describes his mission: "to bring good news to the poor. . . . to proclaim release to the captives and recovery of sight to the blind, to let the oppressed go free, to proclaim the year of the Lord's favor." Inspire giving with stories that communicate the message of the cup of cold water given to "the least of these," described in the parable of the last judgment from Matt. 25:31-46.

When I was a child, I looked forward to the times when missionaries from other nations would speak in our church. Their tales of ministry were exciting and inspirational. Many congregations now hold "Missions Conferences" or "Missions Weekends." They require a lot of work and attention to detail, but the "special events" in the life of the church are excellent opportunities to tell stories. Real people with stories to tell build trust and confidence within the congregation and in the denomination. They personalize the work of the congregation in the world. They help people feel good about giving.

Special offerings provide opportunities to tell stories. They should never be a "hard sell." Each offering has a story. Quite often, denominations send pictures, articles, and other materials to members to help communicate the purpose and intent of the offering.

Some annual offerings are scheduled and are traditional, such as the One Great Hour of Sharing. Others may be spur-of-the-moment, such as flood relief or the church's response to the devastation of an earthquake. The special offering is an opportunity for people to participate directly in something that many of them will feel is important.

Joe Walker counsels, "People want to feel that what they give comes out of a sense of voluntary participation in something because of its intrinsic worth, rather than out of a sense of imposed obligation or duty."[6] Special offerings provide an opportunity for people to give to something that grabs their particular interest.

The appeal is generally appreciated most by baby boomers, baby busters, and those who give little or sporadically. Generous church leaders are more likely to resent special offerings than erratic givers. One reason many people appreciate special offerings is that we often tell stories when the offering is received.

Stories That Give Thanks

All givers want affirmation for their giving. Don't take that to mean that the largest givers should be coddled. Don't give "the best seats in the synagogues and places of honor at banquets" (Mark 12:39) to the largest givers of the church. *Everyone* needs affirmation. If the only place you can affirm some people is in their giving, do it. You are not promising a seat in heaven. You are not even promising a seat on the Administrative Board of the congregation. Simply affirm the generous people for their generosity.

Second, let people know that their giving is making a difference in the church, in the community, and in the world. Tell stories. Weave affirming remarks about the mission and ministry of the congregation and the denomination into the newsletter, business meetings, sermons, and Sunday school classes. An excellent time to tell a story is just before the offering is received in the worship service.

Third, ask generous people to give a personal testimony of their giving journey. Every congregation has people who can relate a story of what giving means to them. No two people have the same story, yet every listener compares his or her own story with the testimony being shared. An inner comparison of the stories provides fertile soil for spiritual growth.

The "Story" in a Chart

Publish a giving profile of your church at least twice a year. The profile may look like one of the two examples on the following page.

<table>
<tr><th colspan="2" style="text-align:center">CHURCH A</th></tr>
</table>

WEEKLY GIFT	# of persons giving at this level
$400 +	1
$250 – $400	3
$150 – $250	7
$100 – $150	9
$ 50 – $100	27
$ 25 – $ 50	32
$ 15 – $ 25	56

CHURCH B

WEEKLY GIFT	# of persons giving at this level
$400 +	0
$250 – $400	1
$150 – $250	0
$100 – $150	1
$ 50 – $100	3
$ 25 – $ 50	6
$ 15 – $ 25	14

The chart is a story that will not communicate to everyone, but it will visually announce giving possibilities to others. Many givers want to know where they fit into the church's story, and the chart helps them know where they are. It calls many persons to recognize that they are able to play a different role in the story. It is a method of invitation into the story of giving within a community of Christian people.

Not all giving is listed on the chart. In our larger mythical church above, we list 135 giving units. Twenty-five giving units are listed in the smaller congregation. When asking members to consider moving up a step, the invitation is visually clear on the chart.

Church leaders often ask the question, "What about people who give but are not on the chart?" There seems to be a fear that people will be left out. Experience has shown that this is not a problem. Announce at the beginning that this is a chart of the giving units from $15 per week and up. You may extend the chart down to $5 per week, but nothing is gained by noting that many people in the congregation give $1. Raise the standard of giving rather than blessing low expectations. The primary purpose of the chart is to raise the sights of giving. Publishing the fact that forty people are giving $ .50 a week does not raise sights.

CONCLUSION

Stories communicate truth, while raising the vision of what is possible for the church and for the giver. They provide inspiration and information in ways that capture the imagination of the hearer. Stories are nonthreatening means to help people look at the faith and their own actions from a fresh vantage point.

Stories are appropriate in sidewalk conversations, as well as in formal business meetings. They can be used in devotionals and in sermons. It is to the task of preaching that we turn in the next chapter.

9
PREACHING

"Stewardship is neither management nor mani-
pulation. It is confrontation."[1]

Wallace Fisher
All the Good Gifts

Fisher is right. Stewardship is not manipulation. It is confrontation—
confrontation in the sense that we are confronted by the grace of God that
sets us free to act in ways that bring joy and satisfaction. We are confronted with a decision that we are free to answer with either a yes or a no
(and a lot of possibilities in-between). The confrontation is an invitation
to respond with tangible action, but it is not works righteousness. We are
confronted with a request and a possibility, rather than a heavy weight of
requirements.

Many pastors are convinced that church members look for excuses to
stay away from worship on "Stewardship Sundays." Some pastors would
like to stay away on that Sunday also. If a visitor shows up when a sermon focuses on giving, the pastor is doubly embarrassed. Lay members
are apt to apologize to the newcomer and assure him or her that "this was
not a normal Sunday." It doesn't have to be that way. Preaching about
giving can be an "upper" instead of a "downer."

Brian Bauknight affirms the "unalterable conviction that finances and
the issues of money should be raised without apology or hesitation. They
are an integral part of the meaning of discipleship."[2] Preachers need not
dread the stewardship sermons. The week of preparation can be a time of
excitement rather than agony.

In the fall of 1993 my wife and I attended a worship service in a large
New York City church. The sermon was filled with shoulds, oughts, and
you-need-to's. After twenty minutes of being shoulded and oughted, I was
worn out and (almost) depressed. The sermon was about giving of one's
time in ministry. I would hate to think of what that pastor would do with a

sermon on giving! Let preaching for giving sing! Fill the sermons with joy! Open the doors of a new world of giving for the hearer, while confirming the joy for those in the congregation who have discovered the joy already.

A few years ago my wife and I went to India. The problems in that country seem overwhelming. Seventeen different languages are spoken. A large percentage of the people cannot read or write. One out of every seven people living on planet Earth lives in a nation about half the geographic size of the United States of America. The population of India is increasing annually by over 14 million. It is growing at a rate equal to the entire population of Australia every year. They have an upper class and a sizable middle class, but the numbers of poor seem astronomical.

Many North Americans who go to India get depressed. The needs are so great, and the resources so limited. We tend to throw up our hands and say "What's the use?" Guilt is produced, but no action follows.

The Indian Christians we met on our trip refuse to look at what they can't do or at what they "ought to" do. They simply do what they *can* do. They feel that they are free to use their limited resources to make the best of each situation. They offer whatever they have with the trust that God can magnify the loaves and fishes. Giving becomes an act of freedom, rather than an obligation or duty. Their giving is in response to the God of love, rather than a duty to a demanding God.

The Indian experience is a reminder of basic Protestant theology. We affirm that God cannot be bought. God's grace is freely given. We are free to respond. Giving because we ought to give is joyless. The remedy is an invitation into a great and joyous partnership with a loving, serving God. We give—not to merit God's approval—but to respond to God's mercy.

Stewardship preaching is a call to the central motifs of the gospel. It is grace-filled preaching. It is confrontation by invitation rather than obligation. It calls for free response. Preaching about giving invites people to accept the worth that is declared upon them by God. Joy comes from acceptance of that worth, instead of seeking worth through stocks, real estate, prestige, or other accumulated wealth. If our real worth comes from God, we are free to share of the treasures of this world.

Any preacher (lay speaker or ordained clergy) who has a word processor is encouraged to use the "Go Find" button. After the sermon is written, ask the computer to find every use of the words *ought, should, must,* and *need to.* Replace each use of the obligatory words with words that more appropriately communicate the gospel. Use words that invite rather than burden.

A fundamental question is: "Why preach about giving?" The answer comes from the testimony of scripture. We would have to ignore much of the Bible if we were going to say nothing about money and possessions. From Genesis through the New Testament, the witnesses told stories of their struggle with economic justice and charitable sharing. They supported the institution (the Temple), and they looked out for those who were shut out of the economic system. *Widows* and *orphans* were the code words for those at the bottom of the economic pecking order. The word *homeless* fills that role in our day. Jesus told parables about payment for workers (Matt. 20:1-16), investments (Matt. 25:14-30), and economic justice (Luke 16:19-31). Paul wrote letters to encourage giving to help the poor (2 Cor. 8 and 9). The Epistle of James links faith and economic justice together in clear, no-nonsense language. Giving is always within the context of a person's stewardship of all resources. A Bible without the passages about money, economics, and possessions would be a very short book. A year of sermons that ignores these passages shortchanges the people.

Early church leaders wrestled with issues of charity and economics. Martin Luther protested against the sale of indulgences. He considered it a heretical method of solving the church's need for funds. John Wesley preached several sermons on a lifestyle of giving and lived the life he preached.

Few people in North America at the end of the twentieth century would claim that families and individuals "have it together" financially. Bankruptcies are filed every day by people who were once "worth millions" and by others who never got out of the financial hole. The Gross National Product of both the USA and Canada are increasing, yet many people are out of work. Assurances from government leaders that the economy is growing give little comfort to the wage earner who has just been laid off. No aspect of life touches the emotions more deeply than money issues. We are super-sensitive. It is the primary taboo subject. The biblical heritage calls us to face taboo subjects with the unique perspectives of the faith.

Salaries and resources are common symbols of a person's worth in our culture. People who just barely scrape by at jobs paying small wages or who are on public assistance have a difficult time feeling good about themselves. Unfair and unhealthy methods of compensating compound the problems.

People with substantial resources may "think of themselves more highly than they ought to think" (see Rom. 2:3) Others with large incomes or considerable resources may feel guilty and burdened by the weight of responsibility for their assets. The gospel can have a profound, positive effect on the lives of people when the grace-given resources of God guide our personal and community economic decisions. Many other economic tugs and pulls create havoc. People hurt. People hunger to hear the Good News that they can be defined as ones loved by God, rather than primarily identified by their possessions or lack of possessions. Address the hurt through the message and the spirit of the gospel. It is a freeing message.

Preaching on giving is more than getting funds to keep the church going. In fact, the church budget is not the central issue. Justice and righteousness are matters of the connection between life and the God of the gospel. People who find giving to be joyful experience a new dimension of life that is liberating. A shalom (peace) comes when acquisition is replaced by sharing as the dominant motivation.

THEOLOGY AND STEWARDSHIP PREACHING

Theology is part of one's homiletic approach to financial stewardship. To oversimplify, if the one who preaches believes that people should be divided simplistically into two distinct classes—those who give and those who don't—the sermon will be proclaimed in a way that communicates the theology. We could diagram this theological stance in the following manner.

out	in

The theology is static. People are either in or they are out. They are either givers or they are not. At the extreme, they are either saved or they are damned. A preacher with this theological stance will address the "In" folks in one way and the "Out" folks in another. Every person in the congregation will know which he or she is. In this theology, only "real" Christians can be giving Christian stewards.

All of us who are church leaders are tempted to judge people by their giving. The tithers are assumed to be the *real* Christians. People who never give or who give very little are deemed to be out of relationship with God. The in/out theology lends itself to lecturing from the pulpit. Guilt trips are laid on those who believe they are in (but are not giving generously), and shame is offered to the non-giver.

The story Jesus told about two men who went to the temple to pray exposes the grave danger of in/out theology. The man who thought he was "in" bragged about the fact that he fasted twice a week and gave away a tithe of his income (see Luke 18:9-14). The other man had nothing to brag about. He could only cry, "God, be merciful to me, a sinner!" (v. 13). Jesus said, "This man went down to his home justified rather than the other" (v. 14).

An alternative theological model might be diagrammed in the following manner:

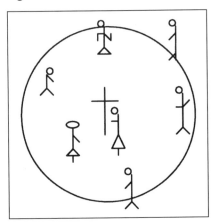

The circle represents the whole family of faith, the household of God. In this diagram, we see that some people who relate to the community of faith are just barely within the circle. Others have matured. They are close to the center, who is Jesus Christ. All are part of God's family.

People who are justified still need God's work of sanctification. Acceptance of the forgiving love of God in Jesus Christ does not mean that God is finished with us. We still have the need and opportunity to grow toward greater faithfulness.

If a person has just placed her toe into the Christian community, we do not condemn her because she is not at the center. Instead, we lovingly nurture the pilgrim and promise to accompany her on the journey. A friend looked at this diagram and said, "I don't care where they are in the circle. The important thing is which way they're facing."

Some theological language talks about accepting people where they are but not leaving them there. We are all pilgrims. We have not arrived. Most congregations have the whole range of pilgrims. Some have barely put their toe into the water. Some are rigorously training for the marathon. Preaching has a challenging and affirming word to say to people wherever they are in their faith journey.

We cannot expect people who have been outside the fold to immediately become generous givers because they have formally united with the church. We can expect that they will *move toward* generosity. Spell out the expectation with clarity. That is a job of preaching. Don't be apologetic. *Giving* is a good word. Use it with assurance and joy.

Possessions and faith cannot be left separate. Jesus said, "Where your treasure is, there your heart will be also" (Matt. 6:21). Faith that is separated from economics is an incomplete faith. People who do not apply faith convictions to the way money is earned, saved, given, and spent are on shaky spiritual and moral ground. People working on the connections between what they believe and what they do are growing Christians.

It is my contention that giving is part of what it means to be a Christian. The person who has nothing to give is in need of justice and mercy. A Christian who has something to give and withholds it all is, at best, an ailing or immature Christian. In Acts 5:1-11, we find the uncomfortable story of Ananias and Sapphira. They sold a plot of ground and apparently claimed that they were turning over all the proceeds to a fledgling Christian community; however, they held back some of the money.

It is not clear that there was anything wrong in withholding some of the money, but to misrepresent their commitment was an abomination that led to their death. Their story immediately follows the story of Barnabas who sold a field and brought the money to the apostles. Apparently, Ananias and Sapphira wanted the honor and prestige without the cost. By trying to live a lie, they lost everything—especially the joy of giving.

Preaching on giving requires openness and honesty. It may take a lot of practice for some people to become open without sounding like bragging. Ordained clergy are as likely to have a problem with speaking about giving as any laypersons. It is a spiritual issue for the clergy as much as it is for laypersons. Discussions with a trusted friend can help clergy talk about the meaning and power of money in their own lives. Few people can be effective in preaching about giving until they have discovered the joy of generosity themselves.

WHEN TO PREACH ABOUT GIVING

When should we preach about giving? Two responses normally come to that question. The first is: "I never preach about stewardship." The second response is: "Stewardship is a part of every sermon I preach." Did you notice that the question was about giving but the answer usually comes in terms of *stewardship*?

To the extent that stewardship is about our response to God through the use of our time, talent, and resources, as well as our care for the creation, relationships, and influence in the world, every sermon is a stewardship sermon. Giving is more specific. If every sermon urged people to give generously, preachers would sound like the religious programs on television that spend half of their time pleading for funds.

At the same time, preaching for giving is appropriate any time of the year. Because people are receptive to new ways of looking at their commitments at times other than the annual financial campaign, it is well to include giving as part of the invited response at any appropriate time throughout the year. Whenever the text suggests giving, it is appropriate to preach on giving. Advent and Epiphany sermons can hardly ignore giving. Advent focuses on the gift of God's Son, Jesus Christ, in the world. Epiphany remembers the world coming to Jesus as symbolized by the magi who brought gifts to the Christ child. Passages from the scriptures that call us to justice usually have an economic dimension. Giving is one part of the economic response we make to the confronting love of God.

Every giving sermon is in the context of the whole ministry of the church and the whole commitment of the person. If preaching becomes separated from the mission of the church or the holistic response of the person, it degenerates into manipulative fund raising and brings shame to the church, to the preacher, and to the faith. Preach giving with joyful and holy boldness. The sermon is an opportunity to invite people into a deeper relationship with God and with all God's creatures and creation through giving.

How to Preach about Financial Stewardship

Lovingly — Love may be enthusiastic exhilaration, or it may be "tough love" that says no as well as yes. Care for people is communicated by countenance as well as by words. Some people in the pews hurt because of financial problems, either of their own doing or due to unavoidable circumstances. The important thing to remember is that some are experiencing a rough time financially. It is hard for people to cope with adversity when more burdens are placed on them by their church.

Even in a church where the overall level of giving is low, some people give generously. Others are taking steps toward greater generosity. Affirm the steps people take, even though they have not arrived at their destination. In what direction are they heading? Giving is not a healthy subject to address in a sermon when anger or frustration places a barrier. A congregation can sense whether the confrontation is in love or in anger. Preach about giving *because* you care about the people.

Positively — In any congregation many people feel burdened with money problems. When giving is communicated in a negative manner, the burden is heavier. People come to church to hear the Good News. Giving is within the context of the gift of love named Jesus. Giving preaching is not positive thinking but *positive response* to the positive action of God in Jesus Christ. It is forceful without being flippant.

Testimonies to the joy of giving and to the joyous results of giving provide support for the giver and encouragement to grow as a giver. A story about the way a certain ministry supported by the congregation has helped people will affirm the giver. It is a legitimate reward. Even a story of failure, if told with compassion, can be told affirmatively. After all, not every investment pays the dividends we hoped for, but that is OK. The sharing of disappointments is a kind of affirmation.

I receive a monthly newsletter from a ministry with the homeless. Stories of ministry with the people that come through the doors of Community Care Fellowship are usually openended. I read of frustration and hope. The writers know how to share frustration in a positive manner. The articles communicate the assurance that God is part of the ministry, even when the outcome is not as we hoped. The articles encourage me to continue to contribute time and money to that ministry.

Healthily — Guilt often spills out when money is mentioned, whether this was intentional or not. The world around us has an unhealthy relationship with money and possessions. The church has the opportunity to proclaim that we can take charge of our possessions through the power of God in Jesus Christ. Our possessions (or our debts) do not need to control us. Preaching for giving is a proclamation of health in a hurting world.

Nothing can be more freeing to many people in our culture than to discover that meaning in life is not determined by economic standards. The sword is double-edged. If there are those in the congregation who believe that their place in life (and life everlasting) is assured by fiscal success, the preached word is a call to repentance. If the culture has proclaimed to people that they are of little worth because they have few possessions, the same word says to them, "You are people of great worth in God's sight."

Humorously — Any mention of money tends to make North American listeners get tense. Humor is disarming; it punctures pretensions. The preacher can "play the fool" about money and giving. Stories in which the storyteller is the "goat" often help a congregation relax. Humor is useful but is to be used wisely. Satire often disparages people and has no place in effective preaching. Humor is to lift up rather than to put down.

One of the best practitioners of healthy humor in preaching is Brian Bauknight, pastor of Bethel Park United Methodist Church in Pennsylvania. He says, "Good stories, in addition to humor, are integral to good preaching."[3] He recommends that pastors avidly collect cartoons and humorous stories that help illustrate the joys and opportunities of spiritual growth through giving.

Passionately — All preaching should be passionate. Unless the preacher believes what he or she says and is enthusiastic about it, little change is likely to take place in the life and practice of the hearer. New ways of acting are *caught* more than they are *taught*. Let preaching be a time when there is good news to catch. People rarely respond to a dry lecture—no matter how true the words may be.

With Commitment — Finally, preaching asks for commitment. Preaching is not an academic lecture about giving. Rather, it is a call to enter the joyful pilgrimage of giving or to growth in giving. A campaign sermon (the horse) focuses on commitment to a budget. The "tractor" of giving focuses on giving as spiritual pilgrimage.

Many years ago I attended a workshop on preaching in Seymour, Indiana. While leading the workshop, H. Eddie Fox asked the participants to bring a statement of purpose to the next session. When the next session began, he asked if any of the participants would be willing to read their statement of purpose to the whole group. The second person who volunteered said, "My sermon is about. . . ." Eddie almost shouted back, "I did not ask you to tell me what the sermon was about. I asked what the *purpose* was."

The purpose of preaching on giving is commitment to Jesus Christ. Preaching for giving lifts up one discipline related to that commitment. Some people "give" themselves into deeper commitment. Other people commit and begin to give more fully. We do not program response. The purpose of preaching for giving is to invite commitment in whatever manner God will lead.

10
THE INVITATION

A farm equipment dealer described a beautiful new tractor in the showroom to the farmer who was looking at it. Lavish words painted an exciting picture of power coupled with ease of operation. Each special feature was eloquently enhanced with sales hyperbole. Glowing terms were used to proclaim the wisdom of investment in this particular model. Then the dealer told the farmer how much he (the dealer) needed to make this sale. If the farmer didn't buy the tractor, the company might go out of business!

Too often, this story is similar to what happens in our churches. Actually, it may be *better* than what we do in the church. Ministries of the church can be described in a vivid way to excite the potential giver. Features of the church's ministry are seldomly extolled. In a rapid move, we zero in on the invitation: "Please give, because the church needs the money to keep going." It is not an invitation that inspires.

The invitation is not an invitation to keep the church afloat but to participate in its mission. Education about the mission and ministry of the church and about giving is not enough. Inspiring invitations are challenging and essential to generous giving! The invitation is to invest in gospel work in this world.

It is time for the church to give straightforward invitations to give. People being invited to give want direct talk. Nervously dancing around the invitation feels like an apology to the potential giver. If the church has to apologize for asking people to give, the hearer assumes that the cause isn't very important. The uneasiness may even raise doubts about the legitimacy of the invitation.

Jesus issued clear, no-nonsense invitations. "Come, follow me" (Luke 18:22) was a dramatic, life-changing invitation to commitment. It was clear and to the point. He challenged a wealthy young man: "Go, sell what you own, and give the money to the poor; . . . then come, follow me" (Mark 10:21). Those who heard Jesus had no doubt about what he was asking. The hearer had an opportunity to say yes or no. Potential followers were cautioned to "count the cost" (Luke 14:28, NKJV). Jesus didn't give folks ideas to ponder; he confronted them with the invitation to live on new terms.

Though frightening to many people, commitments are virtually inescapable. Every contract is a commitment. A marriage ceremony marks the commitment of two people to one another. Each use of a credit card is an implied commitment among the buyer, the seller, and the credit card company. Athletes make a commitment to the team's training program. Young men and women who enlist in the military make a commitment for a certain number of years. Commitments are a part of life.

Not all invitations are worthy of our commitment. Jesus told a parable about people who received an invitation to a banquet. All had prior commitments. One had recently gotten married; another had bought a work animal; and the third had just purchased a tract of land (Luke 14:15-24). They were committed, but their commitments were getting in the way of a higher commitment. At least, they all knew what they were being invited to attend. Their decision to say no carried its own consequences.

We receive an abundance of invitations each day. Some are accepted more consciously than others; some are easy to ignore; some are taken more seriously than others. The consequences of some decisions we make concerning invitations are more significant than for others. Few of us spend a lot of time cataloguing our invitations or listing our commitments to see if they are worth our time and energy—whether they are worth our lives.

Datebooks and calendars indicate time commitments. They are symbols of a response to an invitation. Credit card reports and canceled checks provide a fairly clear picture of our financial commitments. They are a response to advertising or to a felt need. They indicate more than our purchases. In a capitalist economy, the places where we spend our money announce what is important to us. Our expenditures are symbols of our commitments.

Giving is only one kind of invitation the church offers. It is a *part* of commitment but not *all* of it. In a culture with such strong economic implications for every action, giving is a very important dimension. It is a powerful sign—both to the outside world and to the self-understanding of the giver.

The cultural taboo about money is most evident when church people talk about giving. Some people have no problem inviting others to make a commitment to recycle. Some will invite people to buy a season ticket to support an athletic team or the symphony. Pastors may invite people to make a commitment to Jesus Christ at the close of a worship service. The invitation to give scares people who are at ease asking for other kinds of commitments.

It is time to make an invitation to give as natural as any other invitation to commitment. It is important to the life of the giver and to the ministry of the gospel. If practice is required, let us practice. If therapy is needed for the health of our spiritual lives and the mission of the church, let us seek therapy!

JESUS AND GIVING

An invitation to commitment to Jesus Christ as personal Lord and Savior includes commitments of time and money. Stress and distress increase when life separates into compartments that fail to communicate and coordinate. "No one can serve two masters" (Matt. 6:24). No one can serve *one* master without the support of a community. Jesus did not stop with the words "Go, sell what you own." He also said, "Come, follow me" (Luke 18). He offered support of the community along with the invitation for the man to change his economic circumstances. The call to commitment by the church must be accompanied by an offer of support.

Jesus had a lot to say about the way we manage our resources. He recommended sharing, giving, and sacrificing. He believed that the way we use our resources reflects our relationship with God.[1] The church's invitation to commitment is always in the context of the mission of Christ. Financial giving is one dimension of the committed life. To omit giving from the commitment invitation is to ignore an important part of our faith response.

FIRST STEPS

A farmer may be afraid to invest thousands of dollars in a new tractor. I remember the fear I felt the first time I bought a car. What would happen if I could not afford the $173? Ambivalence is normal. "I want to but I don't dare," is a commonplace emotional reaction. The same tensions are common when people are invited to become giving people. The decision to begin on the giving route is not easy.

For years the church has emphasized recruiting members instead of conversion. We try to add to our rolls by receiving the children of members and "stealing sheep" from other parishes. The emphasis on giving has been almost entirely on encouraging increases by those who already give. A generation is coming into the church today that has no experience in giving. We must learn to talk unashamedly about a commitment to become giving people to those who have no experience with the idea.

Just as a salesperson may invite the farmer to take a test drive on the tractor, church leaders find it helpful to invite people to "try out" giving. For many, the act of giving is a major new venture in life. It is a significant step in personal growth and spiritual development. It is our task to encourage those first steps, even if they are far below the potential of the person seeking to become a giver. Affirm people where they are, while encouraging them to move ahead. Invite "in season and out of season." Invite whenever there is opportunity. Don't wait for an annual campaign.

Many church leaders began giving as small children and now give a tithe or more. They often have a difficult time understanding how a small gift can be significant for a person who has never grown up with the practice. It is. It is a very big step for many people. Development officers know that almost all large-gift benefactors started out with small gifts to their foundation or institution. Rarely does a new Christian begin by giving $200 or more a week.

Our invitation to all people is (1) to start (or continue) a commitment to give and (2) to channel the giving through the church. There is no need to apologize for an invitation to commit a portion of one's financial resources to the ministry and mission of the church. If we believe it is important for people to give and that the mission of the church is important, the invitation to give can be extended with excitement, energy, and conviction.

The Return on Investment

Working with a realtor, a young couple found a starter home. The down payment and closing costs totaled more than they had in the bank. They had sufficient income to make the mortgage payments but had to ask one set of parents for funds to bring to the closing. The mortgage company said, "If you get the money from your parents, you must have a *gift letter*." The letter would serve as a legal document stating that the money did not have to be paid back.

A gift requires nothing in return. It is based on a relationship but is not a legal transaction. There is no *quid pro quo*. A gift may *evoke* a response, but it does not *require* a response. In fact, a response to a gift is a gift.

A representative of a major industrial manufacturer makes a large donation to the reelection campaign of a politician. Is it a gift? It may be tax deductible as a business expense, but only the most naive would claim that the donor has no expectations of the official. A law recently passed by the

United States Congress requires the return of certain reelection campaign funds if a politician decides against running for office again. This law recognizes that such funds are an investment by the donor (company or individual) in the future—not a gift to a person who happens to be a politician.

A giving commitment is not a sales transaction where the value to be received is balanced by the cost. There is no demand for return. It is an act of faith. At the same time, a reward is expected. The reward is not increased riches, but a life of faith, hope, love, and joy (1 Cor. 13). These benefits are gifts that make a difference rather than a monetary *quid pro quo*.

There are many motivations behind giving. Some sinister methods work. The church's task is not to discover what will work in order to keep the organization afloat. Our task is to mobilize the good motivations within each person to help all the people become giving human beings.

Giving is not a way to buy the goodwill of God. God loves us even if we are not generous. Neither is generosity proof that we are faithful to God. It only proves that we are generous. In the Gospels, we read of Jesus' condemnation of generous givers (tithers) who bragged in the temple (Luke 18:10-14) and who gave generously but did not practice justice toward their neighbor (Matt. 23:23).

Our giving is a free response to a God who has given freely. The only fitting response is a gift with no strings attached. In his wonderful fundraising letter to the churches in Corinth, Paul says, "This is not a command." The appeal for funds for the poor in Jerusalem was not a hammer over their heads. God loves us whether we give or don't give. Christian giving is a response rather than a payment. We want people to give for two reasons. First, we believe that giving helps people on their pilgrimage toward wholeness. Second, the institutional church needs the funds in order to carry on its ministry. We are not ashamed of that fact.

The rewards for giving are many-fold. Each giving person has his or her own story. Those stories inspire and encourage. For some, the reward is a feeling of gratitude. For others, it is a spiritual discipline that keeps the person's eye on "whatever is true, whatever is honorable, whatever is just, whatever is pure . . ." (Phil. 4:8). Each giver is entitled to hear the stories of good done with the funds they contribute. Giving does not carry a promise of riches. It does provide its own means of reward.

Whenever the invitation is extended to give, promise them the use of a tool for spiritual growth. Like any other tool, it can also be used for bad purposes. However, if we stayed away from everything with an element of danger, we would miss the joys of life. Even the scriptures can be used by the devil for his own purposes (Matt. 4:1-11).

CULTURAL BIAS

At its roots, giving is countercultural. Greed is much closer to the North American credo. However, the distinctiveness of the call to give is one of the reasons the message can be heard. The culture is shallow. Deep within each person are values that are much more important. According to the Christian faith, the deepest truth about human beings is that they are created in the image of a generous God. Sin has messed up this beautiful image. Still, the image is there and can be restored. Stories of those who give away what they have inspire us all. Mother Teresa is an icon for many more people than is Michael Milken.

The church has an opportunity to proclaim the joy of giving. It is good for people, the community, the nation, the world, and the reign of God. It is a means of sharing with one another. When the church lifts up the joy of giving, it proclaims an alternative. It is an invitation to wholeness.

Native American groups have given us an excellent example. The "Give Away" is a cultural tradition for many tribes and nations. They observe a tradition that honors giving more than receiving. Esteem is granted to those who give generously rather than to those who accumulate massively. This attitude is similar to that of early Christianity. The first-century church remembered that Jesus had said, "It is more blessed to give than to receive" (Acts 20:35).

Giving through the church has an added dimension that is not found in secular charitable giving—a mystical connection. The giver recognizes a connection with the Divine. The gift is an expression of faith. It is not simply paying the bills or meeting the budget of an institution.

One reason for urging giving through the church is that there is no other organization in our society that urges giving for the sake of the giver. Many organizations urge giving, and many do wonderful things with the money. The church is the one organization in our culture that says that giving is blessed regardless of tax benefits or society's needs. It is good *in itself.*

The task of the church is to proclaim its unique story *and* to make the case that the best places to channel the funds that are given are through its mission and ministries. If the church cannot make that claim, it needs to completely redesign its system to accomplish its mission. Never underestimate the importance of the mission of the church to the giver. Apparently, Jesus did not get upset with people who channeled giving through the temple. He praised the woman who placed two small coins in the Jerusalem temple box (Luke 21:1-4). Yet none of the four Gospels record any advice about weekly giving or about annual campaigns for the temple budget.

DIMENSIONS OF GIVING

There are at least three different kinds of giving. The first is *consistent, disciplined giving*. This is the kind of giving most churches invite through their annual campaigns. Consistent giving has the greatest spiritual value for the giver, as long as the amount given is large enough (proportionately) to be recognized. It is the kind of giving Paul counseled to the Corinthians when he said, "On the first day of every week, each of you is to put aside and save whatever extra you earn . . ." (1 Cor. 16:2).

New givers need guidance on the mechanics of going about the discipline of giving. If they wait until the end of the month to see if there is any money left over for giving, the month is almost always longer than the checkbook. Leftover giving is rarely joyful giving. If people are going to enjoy giving, they will learn to give off the top.

The appeal of this book is to look at other times besides the fall season to invite consistent, proportionate giving. The time to start is when people start, rather than at an arbitrarily scheduled annual campaign.

Some congregations have moved their annual campaign to the spring. Most who have done so never want to go back to the fall. However, the spring may be a better time for some and the fall for others. Mid-summer might even be the best for some people. The only way to discover the best time for people is to ask them. The anniversary of when they joined the congregation may be more helpful to the invitation to give than an annual campaign. Meet the needs of the people on their terms so that they can respond out of who they are with what they have to give.

A second kind of giving is the *special purpose gift*, of which there are many different kinds. Some are one-time collections for disaster relief. Others are annual appeals for scholarships, One Great Hour of Sharing, retirement center ministries, and such. The primary reason people give to special appeals is that they have a predisposition to give to that particular cause. The satisfaction comes in giving to affect particular people in a positive way.

Capital funds campaigns represent another kind of special purpose gift. This tradition goes back at least as far as the building of the temple in Old Testament times. Modern capital funds campaigns may be one-time appeals, such as a Miracle Sunday or a three-year pledge campaign.[2] The motivation for giving is likely to be long-term. It is future oriented. People who give want to leave a legacy for generations to follow. They may expect to get some good out of it in their own lifetime, but self-interest is not a primary factor. The membership in growing churches is so mobile that most capital campaign givers will not be in that particular church long enough to reap the full benefits.

A third kind of giving is commonly called *planned giving*. Planned giving funds rarely come out of current income. They are gifts out of accumulated resources, such as wills, estates, stocks, insurance, property, and a host of other options. When a planned gift is given through the church, a significant religious statement is being made. However, a planned gift is rarely made without an invitation. Planned giving rarely reaps a harvest unless there are regular, consistent invitations. Notes in every bulletin and newsletter support seminars, letters, and other kinds of reminders so that people know the church is serious about *helping* them make a planned gift when they are serious about *making* the planned gift.

TITHING

Tithing has had a turbulent history in the contemporary church. The Old Testament tradition was rediscovered around the turn of the twentieth century. Except in a few smaller denominations, the practice had few advocates among most "mainline" Protestant groups for many years. In the last decade of the twentieth century, tithing is being rediscovered.

Tithing roots are grounded in the Israelite history as recorded in the Old Testament. Jacob promised a tithe when he awoke from the dream of a ladder stretching from heaven to earth (Gen. 28:10-22). The tithe was commanded by the Lord through Moses (Num. 18:25-27; Deut. 14:22-29 and 26:11-13). The prophet Malachi accused those who did not tithe of cheating God (3:6-12).

These passages from the ancient scriptures have been used as a legalistic club to demand a particular level of giving. However, even in the Old Testament, the tithe was a symbol of relationships more than a legal charge. The Living Bible's paraphrase of Deuteronomy 14:23c says, "God gave us tithing to teach us to put Him first in our lives." Tithing is a gift to teach us rather than a demand to force us.

The tithe is often an issue of identity. A great temptation hovers like a cloud near the head of the tither. Tithing is a ticket to bragging rights for some people. It is a platform of self-righteousness for others. Neither stance is legitimate, but that does not discount the value of tithing. Note the New Testament incidents when Jesus condemned those who tithed, while advocating the practice (Luke 11:42 and 18:9-14). Tithing is a guide to giving rather than a badge of honor.

In an attempt to steer away from the dangers of legalism and the pride of identity, a few church leaders have either ignored tithing or reacted against it. They usually leave the potential giver with no standard to work toward. Without some guidance, a commitment to giving has no concreteness. Financial commitment without a target number is too vague to be helpful. Tithing is a teaching tool to help us put God first in our lives. It is a destination to aim at and, then, to move beyond.

New Christians, in particular, seem to appreciate having a standard to guide them as they struggle to align their lives with God's will. They rarely start out giving a tenth of their income, but they can start on the path toward that benchmark. Many discover that the journey toward the tithe helps them "put God first in their lives."[3]

OTHER TRADITIONS

The venerable eighteenth-century English churchman, John Wesley, developed a very different standard for measuring the commitment of resources. His first rule was, "Earn all you can." By that he meant that it was proper to earn a living by using one's full mind and strength.

Then Wesley said, "Save all you can." This dictum was his counsel to live as frugally as possible, only spending money on necessities. The giving commitment naturally followed when he said, "Give all you can." For Wesley, that meant that we should give away anything left over after purchasing the necessities. He determined the annual amount sufficient for his needs. Everything he received above that amount was given away. In a letter to Walter Churchey written on June 25, 1777, he said, "In my will I bequeath no money but what may happen to be in my pocket when I die."[4] Giving, rather than accumulation, was Wesley's urging and practice.

Modern Roman Catholic stewardship leaders emphasize "sacrificial giving." By that, they mean that people should give enough to notice the difference in their lives. Giving will be proportionately large enough to require conscious choices. Catholic leaders also urge that tithing be a standard of "sacrificial giving."[5]

Each of the traditions (biblical and modern) presents insights into the discipline of giving. Each will appeal to some people and turn off others. We need appropriate guidelines and benchmarks that will communicate to those who unite with the church today. Explore new times, new places, and new language, but ground it all in the historical faith.

When the invitation is seen as encompassing all of life rather than simply supporting the budget, a call to commitment is appropriate any time during the year. We do not have to wait for an annual financial campaign to point to giving as a legitimate part of the Christian's life.

GRATITUDE GIVING

The invitation to commitment may seem to contradict responsive giving. A responsive giver *looks back with thanksgiving*. Commitment *looks ahead in faith*. Both dimensions are essential. One without the other lacks the fullness and integrity of the whole gospel.

An invitation to give runs the danger of being heard as a call to give *up* something. Peter said, "Look, we have left everything and followed you. What then will we have?" (Matt.19:27). At that moment he could only see what he was giving up, rather than what he had received, was currently receiving, and was promised. Invite people to look ahead to the blessings of the future, rather than looking with longing toward the past. The joyful giver dreams of what will happen because of the gift, rather than dwelling on "what I could have done with the money."

Gratitude giving is future oriented but it is rooted in a prior commitment. We love because God first loved us (1 John 4:10). Joy-filled Christian giving is not likely unless the giver recognizes the gift of God in Jesus Christ. People enjoy giving a gift to someone they love and one who loves them in return. Giving is a sign of a relationship that is rooted in the past and looks forward to the future.

METHODS

A few pastors and lay leaders will claim that they don't need any methods at all. "We don't need to say anything about money. If people get their hearts right with God, the money will flow." I don't believe it. Show me a church where people give generously but no one ever says anything about giving, money, and possessions. Silence is no more viable than the traditional annual financial commitment campaign in helping people grow spiritually. It is not a viable option for funding the future of the mission and ministry of the church.

A focus on the giver rather than on the budget is not a method, but it informs all methods used. It is the soil out of which authentic methods grow. At this time in history, we would do well to place our energy in building up the soil rather than in harvesting a crop. The long-term health of the church depends on a rich soil of faith. Nurture the soil. Develop the giver. In faith, the harvest will come in God's time.

POSTSCRIPT

This book raises serious doubts about the value of a fall financial campaign as a method of seeking commitments. **Let no one hear the call for the replacement of the fall financial campaign as a diminution of the need for commitment.** On the contrary, commitment to the mission of Christ is as important as it ever has been. The issue is not whether commitment is good, but whether the "horse" we have been using is the best way to invite commitment. The fall financial campaign is not the only way to encourage commitments. I leave you with two basic rules:

1. **Don't stop having financial campaigns until you have other pieces in order. The other pieces are:**

   ◇ A high level of Christian community within your congregation

   ◇ A shared vision of the church's ministry and mission in the world

   ◇ Ways to regularly ask for financial commitments and increases in giving

   ◇ A high level of financial commitment from the core leadership

2. **The end of annual financial campaigns for support of the regular ministries of the church does not negate the need and opportunity for special offerings and capital campaigns.**

   ◇ Special offerings provide opportunities for persons to respond to special needs above and beyond their regular giving.

   ◇ Capital campaigns will probably be necessary for major building and denomination cooperative mission projects for the foreseeable future.

Giving money is never a substitute for giving of one's self. However, it is inconceivable for a person with financial resources to give self without sharing the resources with others. Giving through the church is more than charity. It is an act of faith and a symbol of commitment.

If people were willing to channel their financial commitments through the institutional church, the budget problem might be solved—but not the deeper problem. Giving is important regardless of budgets. Giving is integral to faith; it is not an appendage. It is a reflection of our priorities and commitments—not a side commitment. Mobilize the energies and giftedness of the church to work on the core process. Let us be about God's call upon the church for developing, nurturing, and maturing the faith of the people as faithfully as we know how.

NOTES

CHAPTER 1: CAMPAIGNS, STEWARDSHIP, AND GIVING

[1]John L. and Sylvia Ronsvalle, *The State of Church Giving through 1990* (Champaign, IL: Empty Tomb, Inc., 1992), p. 11.

[2]The Methodist Annual Conference was a clergy-only meeting from 1774 until approximately sixty years ago. It now has equal numbers of clergy and laypersons.

[3]*Christian Stewardship and Ecumenical Confrontation* (Published by the Department of Stewardship and Benevolence, National Council of the Churches of Christ in the U.S.A.), p. 84.

[4]Raymond B. Knudsen, *Stewardship Enlistment and Commitment* (Wilton, Connecticut: Morehouse-Barlow, 1985), p. 26.

[5]Lack of institutional loyalty is often cited as one of the hallmarks of the baby boomer generation, those born between 1946 and 1964. For an indepth analysis of the characteristics of this generation, see Craig K. Miller, *Baby Boomer Spirituality: Ten Essential Values of a Generation* (Nashville: Discipleship Resources, 1992). See also William M. Easum, *The Church Growth Handbook* (Nashville: Abingdon Press, 1990), p. 69.

[6]See Matthew 20:1-16 and Luke 16:1-13.

[7]Peter Block, *Stewardship: Choosing Service Over Self-Interest* (San Francisco: Berrett-Koehler Publishers, 1993).

CHAPTER 2: GIVING AND THE CHURCH'S TASK

[1]For a good review of the Deming management philosophy, see Mary Walton, *The Deming Management Method* (New York: Perigree Books, 1986).

[2]See Chapter 7 for a discussion of church offerings.

[3]For a brief description of the biblical roots of tithing, see Norma Wimberly, *Putting God First: The Tithe* (Nashville: Discipleship Resources, 1988). For a longer treatment of the subject, see Douglas Johnson, *The Tithe: Challenge or Legalism* (Nashville: Abingdon Press, 1984).

[4]Jerold Panas, *Mega Gifts: Who Gives Them, Who Gets Them* (Chicago: Precept Press, 1984), p. 69.

[5]Edward W. Uthe, "Attendance, Pledging, Giving" (an unpublished report created

in 1989 for The Evangelical Lutheran Church of America, 8765 West Higgins Road, Chicago, IL 60631-4180).

6Panas, *Mega Gifts*, p. 69.

7Ibid., p. 231.

8The next highest score was 8.1 for "Community responsibility and civic pride." His institutional experts (fund raisers) also ranked "belief in the mission of the institution" as the highest motivation (but with a 7.9 score). Their next highest rating was "great interest in a specific program within the project" which garnered a 7.1 score.

9James D. Anderson and Ezra Earl Jones, *The Management of Ministry: Building Leadership in a Changing World* (Nashville: Discipleship Resources, 1993).

10Easum, *Church Growth Handbook*, p. 118.

Chapter 3: Leadership for Giving

1Thomas R. Hawkins, *Building God's People: A Workbook for Empowering Servant Leaders* (Nashville: Discipleship Resources, 1990).

Chapter 5: New Member Formation

1Edward W. Uthe, "Fundamental Facts about Stewardship in the ELCA" (an unpublished report created in 1990 for The Evangelical Lutheran Church of America, 8765 West Higgins Road, Chicago, IL 60631-4180).

2On October 10, 1993, the congregation moved into their new building.

Chapter 6: Key Moments in the Life of the Giver and of the Church

1"Church Membership Initiative: Narrative Summary of Findings, 1993" (Appleton, Wisconsin: Aid Association for Lutherans, 1993), p. 5.

2Donald W. Joiner, *Christians and Money* (Nashville: Discipleship Resources, 1992).

3An excellent resource for helping youth think through and try on the life of stewardship is Dan R. Dick, *Choices and Challenges: Stewardship Strategies for Youth* (Nashville: Discipleship Resources, 1994).

4*Giving and Volunteering in the United States* (Washington, D.C.: The Independent Sector, 1992), p. 4.

5Many resources are available that address how churches can intentionally help persons with planned giving. A good source of information is the Planned Giving Resource Center, P.O. Box 840, Nashville, TN 37202.

Chapter 7: The Offering

1Patricia B. Jelinek, "The Offering: A Vital Part of Worship," in *Celebrate Stewardship*, Vol. 4, No. 3 (October 1991). *Celebrate Stewardship* is a quarterly article on the subject of stewardship issued by the Office of Stewardship of the General Board of Discipleship, Nashville, Tennessee.

2Jeffrey Jones, pastor of Epworth United Methodist Church, Cockesville, Maryland.

3Timothy Bagwell is pastor of Martha Bowman Memorial United Methodist Church in Macon, Georgia. He gives an excellent account of effective stewardship preaching in his book, *Preaching for Giving: Proclaiming Financial Stewardship with Holy Boldness* (Nashville: Discipleship Resources, 1993).

4Hoyt L. Hickman was a director of worship ministries at the General Board of Discipleship of The United Methodist Church. He is now retired and lives in Nashville, Tennessee.

5Cyril Charles Richardson, *The Church Throughout the Centuries* (New York: Charles Scribner's Sons, 1950), pp. 29-30.

6See pages 46ff. for a discussion of annual giving patterns.

7See Exodus 23:16, 19; Leviticus 2:12, 14; Numbers 18:12- 13; 2 Chronicles 31:5 and other passages.

CHAPTER 8: TELLING STORIES

1Bagwell, *Preaching for Giving*, p. 55.

2Warren J. Hartman, *Five Audiences: Identifying Groups in Your Church* (Nashville, Abingdon Press, 1987).

3Herbert Mather, *Letters for All Seasons* (Nashville: Abingdon Press, 1993).

4Bagwell, *Preaching for Giving*.

5Charlie Shedd, *The Exciting Church: Where They Give Their Money Away* (Waco, TX: Word Books, 1975).

6Joe Walker, *Money in the Church* (Nashville: Abingdon Press, 1982).

CHAPTER 9: PREACHING

1Wallace Fisher, *All the Good Gifts* (Minneapolis: Augsburg Publishing House, 1979).

2Brian K. Bauknight, *Right on the Money: Messages for Spiritual Growth Through Giving* (Nashville: Discipleship Resources, 1993).

3Ibid., p. viii.

CHAPTER 10: THE INVITATION

1See Matthew 6:1-4, 19-21, 24; Luke 12:13-21, 33-34; 14:28-33; 16:9-15; 18:18-30; 19:1-10.

2For an excellent description of Miracle Sunday, see Wayne K. Barrett, *The Church Finance Idea Book* (Nashville: Discipleship Resources, 1989), p. 95.

3See Wimberly, *Putting God First: The Tithe*.

4John Wesley, *Selected Letters of John Wesley*, ed. Frederick C. Gill (New York: Philosophical Library, 1956), p. 175.

5This was the message I heard while attending the National Catholic Stewardship Conference in Nashville, Tennessee, October 18-20, 1993.